THE ZEN OF
LISTENING

THE ZEN OF
LISTENING

MINDFUL COMMUNICATION IN THE AGE OF DISTRACTION

REBECCA Z. SHAFIR, M.A. CCC

A publication supported by
THE KERN FOUNDATION

Quest Books
Theosophical Publishing House
Wheaton, Illinois ◆ Chennai (Madras), India

The Theosophical Society in America acknowledges with gratitude the generous support of the Kern Foundation in the publication of this book.

First Quest Edition 2000
Second Edition 2003

The Theosophical Publishing House
P. O. Box 270
Wheaton, IL 60189-0270

A publication of the Theosophical Publishing House, a department of the Theosophical Society in America

Library of Congress Cataloging-in-Publication Data

Shafir, Rebecca Z.
The zen of listening: mindful communication in the age of distraction / Rebecca Z. Shafir. — 1st Quest books ed.
    p. cm.
"Quest books."
Includes bibliographical references (p.).
ISBN 0-8356-0826-3
1. Listening. I. Title.

BF323.L5 S53 2000
153.6'8—dc21

00-031759

First Quest Hardcover Edition 2000
Quest Hardcover ISBN 0-8356-0790-9

6 5 4 3 2 1 * 03 04 05 06 07 08

Printed in the United States of America

Table of Contents

Preface to the Second Edition

Since the publication of *The Zen of Listening* in 2000, numerous readers and students from all over the world have been kind enough to share their *eureka!* listening moments with me. It gives one hope to know that the so-called "simple" act of listening can engender profound personal change in transforming a business, reconnecting an adult child with his estranged parents, and saving marriages. And yet such benefits occur every day to people when they choose to listen to each other in mindfulness.

Take Evelyn, for example: a young, talented lawyer from Los Angeles who felt that the adversarial process of litigation was making her, in her words, "confrontative not only in the courtroom, but in the bedroom as well." She became the object of disciplinary action at her law practice for "client negligence." Shocked by this accusation— after all, she put in over sixty hours a week for the practice—she sat through a kind but reprimanding lecture by a partner in the firm. Complaints included not returning phone calls; moreover, when she did, clients felt that she distanced herself from their pain. Associates felt she talked too much and listened too little. Unable to shake the do-or-die mentality when she was at home, Evelyn received similar feedback from her husband and friends. Her righteous, self-serving attitude was creating a gradual disconnection between her and her loved ones. She was becoming scattered and irritable. When her husband faced her with the prospect of divorce, Evelyn woke up.

She started taking yoga classes on the weekend. A friend in her class—a fellow attorney who had traveled a similar path—gave her *The Zen of Listening*. Evelyn began introducing mindful minutes into her day. Over the next several days, she began to appreciate how her boss tended to his clients in a way that didn't leave him exhausted, frustrated, or angry when he went home. She noticed how listening more and allowing some silence helped her get a palpable sense of her clients' real interests in solving their dilemmas. This insight led her to envision more creative and amicable solutions for them. As Evelyn recently reflected, "Mindful listening put my life in balance."

Clifford, a forty-two-year-old single man who lives in Chicago, used to dread visiting his elderly parents. Without fail, after the usual small talk about work and the weather, his parents always seemed to sneak in some advice and suggestions for helping him find a nice girl, getting married, and raising a family. Clifford, through mindful listening practice, was able to put aside his anger; instead, he saw his parents' nagging as their way of helping him find happiness in the only way they knew how. Rather than storm out of the house as he used to, leaving behind bad feelings, Clifford learned to set aside his defensiveness and accept his parents' concern for him. He listened in mindfulness and thanked them for their suggestions. Delighted that they had been heard, his parents were able to hear Clifford's side. Even if they could not accept his life choices, they agreed that preserving their relationship was more important.

Daniel, a minister from Adelaide, Australia, began teaching mindful listening in his marriage counseling sessions. "Learning to listen is the first rule of love," he noted to me. "Listening to oneself helps one make the right choices. Without whole-hearted, selfless listening to your spouse, there is no respect. And without respect, there is no happiness in marriage. The hardest part was getting these young adults to sit quietly and think about someone else besides himself or herself." Daniel was able to accomplish this aim by bringing other adults into the sessions—people who were either in the same age group as his young congregants or slightly older—to share their marital problems and regrets. These counseling sessions grew larger and became more popular. "Before you knew it, people were bringing food and making new friends. . . . Helping others through tough times: that's what listening is all about."

I also want to share a personal story with you that strikes me as an apt metaphor for the process of mindful listening. Some of my clients and I recently took a trip to a postcard-perfect uninhabited isle in the Caribbean. Deemed a "must-visit" destination on our travel map, the island with its captivating beauty seemed designed to lull visitors into a hypnotic state of tranquility.

Once we had gotten past the confectioner's sugar-like sandy beaches, our guide led us through a tropical palm forest dripping overhead with vines of succulent orange flowers. Tiny painted lizards and gekkos scurried across the not-so-well beaten path, which turned quickly into a treacherously steep trail lined with wild cacti. My hitherto dreamy state of consciousness began to dissipate, especially upon hearing the distant sound of a rhythmic, low, thunderous boom—a curious intrusion to the sweet trills of the little purple birds that had welcomed us to this paradise just minutes ago. We ascended the narrow hilly path, treading carefully upon the slippery rocks and linking hands for support on the steeper parts. Clearly, this hike required more climbing traction than my weatherbeaten flip-flops could provide. Wishing I had better prepared myself for the terrain, I leaned against a prickly cactus tree, removed the sandals, and caught up with the group. My arms and back did *not* emerge from the prickly encounter unscathed.

Several minutes later, as we neared the top, the thunderous beats pulsed even louder. When we reached the precipice, our conga line came to a halt. Our guide yelled, "Hold on . . . and look *down!*" Just as he spoke, a gust of wind swept us with a spray of water droplets that richocheted upwards from the five-hundred-foot drop to the dark, ferocious, rocky shore below. Stunned and breathless, we gripped the narrow strip of earth on all fours and stared awestruck at the shocking but spectacular show of nature's fury—a sight unimaginable to any beachcomber just a half mile back.

So how does my adventure tie into the process of mindful listening? Sometimes we get complacent in relationships. We allow comforts and stock options to lull us into a false sense of stability, often ignoring the subtle signs of disconnection that signal caution ahead. At other times, the warning signs of a breakdown in a relationship are clear, but we are mentally ill-equipped to turn things around. Quite often our suffering is the product of our own making: hyperactive schedules, status consciousness, prejudice, and self-interest. The scariest part for some of us is peering over that cliff and deciding it's time to make some internal changes, to ground ourselves in truth and integrity or else slip into the abyss.

Listening is a skill we need to take seriously in this Age of Distraction, no matter what our occupation, creed, or culture. Mindful listening can bring about unexpected discoveries, make visible the invisible, and change us in profound ways. This whole-body listening approach requires an adventurous, curious spirit and courage to confront and dissolve the obstacles that keep us from connecting with each other in peace and harmony. So don your gear, take a deep breath, and get ready to enjoy the journey . . . cacti and all!

Acknowledgments

I bow humbly to the people who taught me the power of mindful listening and helped bring this book into being. To Michelle Lucas, who taught me that a support group is for listening, not lecturing. To the staff and students at The Boston Center for Adult Education, who believed that a different approach to the teaching of listening could work! To my martial arts teachers who, through sweat and tears, taught me that the real strength lies in a focused mind. To Jane Sokol Shulman, audiologist Nancy Cohen, and my patients, who awakened in me the appreciation for the renewal that comes from loss.

To the physicians at Lahey Clinic, particularly Dr. Frank Scholz, Dr. Prather Palmer, and Dr. Stephen Kott, who continue to teach the meaning of a good bedside manner.

To the many supporters and nurturers, including Morty and Barbara Eagle, Patty Brent, all my friends from the Greater Lowell Road Runners and Winchester Highlanders, who prove every day that listening is a part of good health.

A bow to Marcia Yudkin, writer, marketer, mentor, and friend, who gave shape to my writing and enthusiastic support throughout the process.

To Shaneet Thompson who shared valuable nuggets about listening from a mediator's standpoint. To Zen Master Bon Hyon who reviewed my manuscript and continues to clarify my understanding of Zen Buddhist philosophy and how it relates to communication.

I am especially grateful for the opportunity to have met so many people through the process of writing this book. To my agent, Susan Schulman, and to Christine Morin for their confidence in me. To Sharron Brown-Dorr, the publishing manager of Quest Books, who helped me focus my vision and bring it forward. To my editor, Jane Lawrence, a soul sister, whose patience and writing skills helped bring the final drafts to a new level of clarity and quality.

My loving appreciation to my mother, Iris, who has always been my inspiration for using my potential in all endeavors; and my father, Paul, who always encouraged me to look for the opportunities and take on the challenges.

To my sisters and brother, who listened tirelessly to me growing up. Now that I'm a bit wiser, I hope I can return the favor.

Thanks to my stepdaughter, Tal, who helps me see equanimity in all things.

To my loving husband, Sasha—soulmate, advisor, and technical guru—thank you for your unselfish support and guidance in making this book a reality.

And, finally, to my loyal friend and canine companion of thirteen years, Spud, who was the best listener a person could have. Spuddy, this book is for you.

Introduction

*W*elcome to the Age of Distraction! Never before has it been more difficult to get through an average day and feel a sense of accomplishment. According to Kirsten Downey Grimsely ("Message Overload Taking Toll on Workers," *The Washington Post*, May 20,1998), the average worker is interrupted six times every hour. David Shenk, author of *Data Smog* and *Why You Feel the Way You Do,* reports that Americans were exposed to six times as many advertising messages in 1991 as they were in 1971. Shenk claims, "Information overload has replaced information scarcity as an important new emotional, social, and political problem."

Unless we can arrange to live in a cave, there isn't much we can do to eliminate external distractions. In all fairness to the information explosion, it's exciting and convenient to have massive amounts of data accessible with a few keystrokes, and very educational to watch many of the cable TV channels. It's not just the noisy environments, megachoices at the mall, multitasking, information overload, or the intrepid remote control that challenge our ability to listen. It is the internal distractions that threaten our very existence and hopes for a better world—obsession with time, greed for speed and stuff, prejudice and aversion towards people and change, self-consciousness, ego gratification, negative self-talk, extreme preferences, dwelling in the past while obsessing about the future, and working so hard to sustain these beliefs. These are the delusions that endanger our ability to connect with each other, understand each other, and live in harmony.

The noise and distraction brought on by media hype and technology pale in comparison to our internal noise levels. If we could hardwire a speaker system to the brains of people we come in contact with every day, particularly as they try to listen to us, we'd be shocked at the blare of noise, chaos, and negative overtones of the signals emanating from their minds—critical judgments, visual evaluations, self-conscious comments, thoughts of the past or future, and fears of certain topics. Chances are, we might not want to be around a person who thinks such things about us and themselves.

One of the main reasons we listen poorly is because our internal noise levels are so turbulent and obtrusive that they mask most of what others are saying. Only bits and pieces of their message survive the barrage of our mental interference. Just as we have learned to manage external interference by tuning out, it has become somewhat of a challenge to tune in deeply enough to the messages we *need* to listen to—those of family, coworkers, and customers. Misunderstanding, not being heard, and missing key information due to poor listening are at the crux of societal ills. Traditional approaches to listening improvement are usually ineffective because they come from a point of view of altering surface features instead of reshaping the foundation. If we are to end the suffering associated with not listening, we need to dig deeper to get to the source so change can take place.

Many self-help books on personal relationships, negotiation, sales, and customer service tell us that good listening is essential to success in our personal and professional lives, but they do not explain *how* to listen. The available how-to approaches to better listening give you lists of new ways to behave, as if by magic you master techniques and stick with them. Just like after most self-improvement courses, you may try to force new behaviors for a few days, but gradually, because there is no foundation for these changes, your old tendencies to tune people out and repeat mistakes creep back.

Before you spend more time and money on more self-improvement endeavors, ask yourself what it is you hope to gain from reading this book. Here are some realistic expectations:

1) You can expect to start making some changes today in your ability to listen, changes that will outlive the most determined New Year's resolution and that will permeate other aspects of your life that need improvement.

2) You'll find out why, without heavy analysis, you have trouble communicating in some situations, and what you can do about it.

3) You'll find that these changes in the way you listen also *benefit others.*

This sounds like a tall order, but these expectations are not unreasonable. You hold in your hands *The Zen of Listening,* your thoughtful and practical guide to transforming your ability to listen.

I came to write this book for many reasons, and there was an interesting chain of events that led to my discovery of a mind-body link important in enhancing the ability to listen. I must mention here that most of the names of people whose stories I share in this book have been changed for purposes of confidentiality. Others have allowed me to share their identities with you. These people seemed to appear magically in my life as a way of teaching me the true meaning of listening.

As a speech/language pathologist for twenty years, I worked with adults with impaired ability to communicate due to stroke, head/neck cancer, head injuries, or degenerative diseases. I believed that in

3

order to consider myself a *communication specialist*, I would need to continually sharpen my communication skills. Therefore, I took every opportunity to enroll in workshops on listening and speaking. Since these were the same expensive communication classes being taught to companies and large corporations, I figured they had to be effective. To my dismay, all of the listening classes stressed only the *mechanics* of good listening, so as a conscientious student, I amassed a list of ideas in order to *behave* like a better listener. Whether I was truly listening was debatable. My fellow students also concluded these workshops feeling much the same way I did. As much as we took notes and role played good listening, few of us left the classes thinking that the experience had changed in any meaningful way our ability to listen. My desire to find a more effective way to get people to listen better to each other coincided with a string of events that suggested a possible solution.

At the hospital where I worked, managed care began placing severe restrictions on time spent with patients in order to drive down the cost of health care. For example, if you had a stroke, you would be granted a sixty-day therapy period in which to regain your ability to communicate. In addition, there were pressures to see more patients per day, and that meant more paperwork.

On the plus side, these measures forced me to take a closer look at how I could bring about progress in a shorter period of time with fewer resources. It was a challenge to my flexibility to find a way to keep quality in my work while meeting the economic goals of the hospital.

However, most of my colleagues and I were not eager to embrace a strategy that treated patients as mere statistics. In addition, patients began to feel alienated from their physicians. Could they trust someone who was paid to limit their care? And, from the physicians' point of view (most of whom were schooled in a nonmanaged-care philosophy), what could be considered adequate medical care? The fallout from this necessary evil was disgruntled, sicker patients, stressed-out physicians, and low morale among hospital personnel.

Due in large part to these drastic cost-cutting measures, I saw that I was losing my freshness and enthusiasm in treating patients. My cheerleader style had become dulled by the piles of paperwork and the pressure I had to place on my patients to meet their deadlines for recovery. Since saving money was paramount in this new healthcare environment, I was more reluctant to experiment with innovative methods of treatment, and this squelched my creativity. It was more conservative to stick with what methods usually worked and call it a day. I could sense that my responses were becoming more predictable, and after listening to a tape of myself working with a patient, I discovered that I was lapsing into a robotic response mode. As a means of conserving energy for my other job responsibilities, I found it easier to slot individuals based on age, background, and diagnosis. Aside from the few persons who did not conveniently fit these slots—those who presented some challenges for me—my satisfaction with my work life, once spectacular, had degenerated to merely fair.

Diligent efforts to keep up with the current research in my field and to apply occasional and less costly advances provided periodic sparks. Yet overall I felt frustrated, stagnant, and less fulfilled at the end of a workweek. This exposed an inflexible and self-absorbed side of me. That side fought to survive amid signals that change to a simpler path was imminent.

By my late thirties, I was starting to show the classic signs of burnout. Even my relationships with family were suffering. External amusements such as trendy activities, shopping, money-making endeavors, and competitive sports with the objective of winning became appealing to me. I had become vulnerable to impulsivity, excessive goal setting, accumulation of material things, competitiveness in sports, and advising my siblings instead of just being a good sister—attitudes and behaviors that disconnected me from myself and others. Despite all these self-inflating intentions, there I lay exhausted and unfulfilled after a day of trying to make myself a better person.

Seeking out new career opportunities held promise as a cure for my general malaise, but I had reservations. As many of you have already experienced, financial constraints tempered my impulse to make drastic changes. Instead, my intuition advised me to take a deeper look into myself and the way I related to others before abandoning a life's work for which my talent and personality were well suited. A major rethinking was necessary. I decided that it was worth going on a personal archeological dig to figure out what to do about my situation.

When I was a college student in the seventies, Transcendental Meditation had become a vehicle of self-discovery and a discipline that brought welcome clarity to eighteen credit hours of graduate work and two part-time jobs. Now, once again I began daily meditation. This enabled me to calm my mind and identify the inner obstacles that kept me from working *with* the system instead of against it.

During this renewal phase, I met my husband, Sasha. Aside from his job as a computer engineer, he was a third-degree black-belt martial arts instructor. Watching him, his students, and other instructors practicing various martial arts, I was mesmerized by their concentration and physical control. I admired their balanced state of mind and lack of self-consciousness in daily situations. These people were not monks or part of some spiritual cult, nor was their discipline violent or destructive. They were regular people, who owned businesses or were leaders in their communities. They too faced the same threats of layoff, crazy work schedules, and limited budgets, yet they were at peace with change and used their resources to find creative solutions.

After getting to know these people better, I asked myself, *Is the physical exertion of karate or kung fu the source of this concentration and serenity of spirit? Or is it the focus on quality of movement that improves the ability to attend completely and joyfully to the task at hand?* I believed it was the latter, since I had also observed this mind-body balance in artists, musicians, surgeons, and athletes. While painting, playing, dissecting, or diving, they were all willfully caught in the *flow* of their activities.

Looking back over the years, I recalled several such exhilarating periods of concentrated energy prior to my current burnout period. Many were memorable listening situations. I remember in college being totally absorbed physically and mentally in certain lectures, during medical rounds in my hospital training, or while being critiqued by someone whose opinion I highly valued. I recalled these moments of physical and mental readiness as a relaxed, balanced state, a connectedness between my mind and body. My next question was, *What if this zeal for quality and depth of concentration could be applied to one of our greatest needs, a gift so little used and so often taken for granted—the ability to listen?*

In my search to regain and perpetuate this feeling of connectedness, I enrolled in a martial arts class and studied everything I could find about the mind-body relationship. By getting to know myself painfully through the eyes of my instructors, my reasons for becoming disconnected from my world were made clear. I decided to start over fresh, not by focusing on the results or the outcome of my actions, but with the prospect of being in the moment and discovering the quality in every interaction.

I started to apply this new awareness to what occupied the bulk of my day—*my work as a therapist.* First, during this period of self-awareness, I noticed that when I interacted with patients and coworkers, I became distracted by my own agenda. Assumptions and periods of selective listening led me to miss valuable information. I had become closed within the walls of my routine protocols. In my eagerness to treat the patient, I found myself lecturing patients and their families much too often and asking way too many questions. If they did not comply with my recommendations or the advice of their physicians, I judged them quickly, dismissing their reasons for not following through. I could see how much time was wasted in reinforcing practice, re-explaining, and revising treatment plans. What was at the heart of all this redoing? By not fully listening to the patient or to my own spoken words, I was actually making more work for myself and stalling progress.

Because of my egocentric way of trying to help my patients, it was no wonder why I and so many others left the office exhausted and frustrated most days. I remembered the words of a favorite professor in graduate school that pointed to the importance of listening in a learning situation: "If you do not get to know where that patient is coming from (his background, expectations, etc.) you cannot understand him, and he will not trust your advice."

Little did I guess that my next step toward enlightenment would come from a patient. Just as I was leaving work one day, a weary sixty-nine-year-old man, looking older than his age, stopped me as I closed my office door. He said effortfully, with a tight, twisted face, that he didn't have an appointment, but that he wanted to ask a question. "Sure," I said and brought him into my office. He awkwardly introduced himself as Mr. Hennman; he already knew my name. Mr. Hennman sat down on the edge of his seat, visibly tired from seeing many other specialists that day. At that moment, I had a strange sense that this was not going to be a typical patient visit.

Mr. Hennman told me about his many medical problems and his difficulties expressing himself to others. He hoped that in coming to a communication specialist, I would "just listen." I was somewhat taken aback by his request. After all, wasn't that what I always did ? I put down my briefcase and jacket, sat with my hands on my lap, and looked Mr. Hennman in the eye. He spoke hesitantly, stuttering, looking away at first, and told me how the doctors put so much emphasis on his medical problems, but failed to ask him about *his* main concern, which was his speech. Because he found doctors intimidating (he sensed they were uncomfortable talking with him due to his stutter), he routinely answered in as few words as possible. It took so long to utter a sentence that his doctors often completed his sentences or interrupted him. Mr. Hennman was convinced that his years of indigestion and sleeping problems were in part due to his anxiety about communicating.

Mr. Hennman had a sixth-grade education, had never married, and had worked alone for forty-seven years as a metalsmith. He felt that now it was time to start living his life and learn how to interact with others despite his stutter. Interestingly, as I listened to his story, his speech gradually became less effortful with only an occasional word or sound repetition. His facial contortions eased. He appeared relieved and shocked at the same time as he realized that he had finally been able to express himself fully. Even though Mr. Hennman spoke for only about fifteen minutes, I felt as though I had been swept up in his life and in his remarkable transformation, even if it was only temporary. Now, as if by magic, I was back in my chair. Mr. Hennman thanked me profusely for listening. He felt he would be able to sleep well for once, because someone had taken the time to see his view of things. You can imagine how well I slept that night!

Several days later Mr. Hennman's physician, a doctor from another facility, phoned me and reported that his patient's overall condition had improved considerably following his visit with me. The doctor asked what I had done after years of unsuccessful treatment by his staff. I told him I had done nothing but listen. For the first time, I heard someone blush over the phone.

Mr. Hennman and others like him inspire me daily to extend this experience to others, to study it and teach it. I have had the pleasure of working with many physicians who have taught me the true meaning of the expression "bedside manner." With other doctors, however, I have seen how failure to listen to the patient adversely affects the accuracy of the diagnosis and subsequent treatment. Too often the patient is not given a chance to mention what's on his mind, to share his insight into his health problem. Just as often, due to various communication barriers, a patient does not understand his doctor's explanation of his illness.

Not only good medical practice, but *any* successful business requires optimal listening on both sides of the table. In all industries and, most importantly, in the home, a good bedside manner is the best medicine for solving disputes and getting along with others. Whether we are salespeople, parents, or provide some service, people come to us in need. Quite often they require assistance or are in distress, very much like someone who is ill or dying. They look to trust us in the same way that a patient looks to trust the judgment of a physician. We can all benefit from improving our bedside manner. It does not necessarily mean taking more time, but rather more *willingness to see a situation through the eyes of the speaker.* How can we achieve a positive outcome with each person we come in contact with if our scope is narrowed by self-interest?

My experience as a speech pathologist and my study of psychology, communication disorders, religion, and Eastern philosophy have produced a mindset for listening that I am pleased to share with my students. Judging from their responses, these ideas have been instrumental in shaping their attitudes towards others and their ability to understand and remember what they hear. Most students claim they are happier and more satisfied in their work and family relationships.

From a spiritual and social point of view, listening can be a powerful tool of change. Schoolteachers and counselors, prior to taking my listening class, report their jobs are getting more stressful because they cannot handle the listening needs of their students and clients. If children are not heard by their parents, if their emotional concerns are not taken seriously, they become behavioral problems at home and in the classroom. Hours of TV and video games splinter whatever remains of attention and concentration for schoolwork, and grades suffer. A lack of proper listening role models may lead to frustration, violent outbursts, and loss of self-control. Poor self-esteem cultivated over time leads to substandard performance in the workplace and unhappy family relationships as the ravages of poor listening are handed down to the next generation.

When a person is given a chance to tell his views without the threat of judgment or advice, even if his listener does not agree, that is the first step toward creating good feelings. A sense of openness on both sides allows for discussion and problem solving. Self-esteem grows from the respect that comes from being heard. People are better able to attend to school lessons, projects, and the responsibilities of the workplace when basic emotional needs, like being understood, have been met. Henry David Thoreau said, "The greatest compliment that was ever paid to me was when someone asked me what I thought, and attended to my answer." When confidence grows, we are better able to discover our potential and positively influence others. Mindful listening has the power to change the direction of our lives and those we come in contact with every day.

Listening is also a healthy activity. Studies show that when we listen, heart rate and oxygen consumption are reduced and blood pressure decreases. Contact with others promotes well-being and self-expression, both necessary for good physical health. By being good listeners, therefore, we promote the good health of others by allowing them to reduce their stress and empowering them to solve their own dilemmas. An empathetic listener provides helpful feedback that makes the speaker feel valued. This is a significant gift in a world where the human touch is a rare commodity.

Many of us would like to see an end to discrimination of all kinds, happier families, and a safer, more harmonious future for our children. But how can we as individuals make a difference? We can begin by learning to listen in a *mindful* way. Listening is the first step in making people feel valued. Mindful listening allows us to do more than take in people's words; it helps us better understand the how and why of their views. When understanding occurs, a sense of calm is achieved on both sides, even if no point of agreement is reached. From understanding, respect and trust for one another are possible; we are free to open our minds and widen the scope of potential solutions. Listening is also the first step in any negotiation, whether it means getting your teenager to clean the garage or arranging a cease-fire in the Middle East.

On New Year's Eve 1999, Larry King, on his nightly TV talk show, invited eminent spiritual leaders to share their hopes for the Third Millennium. The Dalai Lama proclaimed the twenty-first century as the "century of dialogue." Evangelist Billy Graham declared that "world peace can come only from the human heart. Something has to happen inside of man to *change our attitude.*"

How do we start changing our attitudes? By listening in a mindful way and becoming aware of what habits we can change today and what habits need to change over time. Sometimes all it takes is someone or something to come our way to make us stop and think about the need to be heard. By taking the ideas in this book to heart, not only will you accomplish more through communicating effectively, but you can begin to make a daily personal contribution to world peace.

Chapter One

Creating a Mindset for Good Listening

If every time we met with someone and
gave them our full and complete attention
for four minutes come hell or high water,
it could change our lives.

—Leonard and Natalie Zunin,
The First Four Minutes

Our goal in becoming mindful listeners is to quiet the internal noise to allow the whole message and the messenger to be understood. In addition, when we listen mindfully to others, we help quiet down *their* internal noise. When they notice that we are totally with them, people feel freer to cut out the layers of pretense to say what's really on their minds. As you read on, you will see mindful listening is a gift not only to yourself, but to others.

It is maddening to think of the knowledge that went in one ear and out the other, the relationships that went sour, or the opportunities missed because we were not better listeners. Over the decades our ability to talk has dramatically surpassed our ability to *listen* to one another. We can easily give someone a piece of our mind, but we have much difficulty taking in another's point of view. We can talk for hours on a given subject, but most of us can retain only a small fraction of a professor's lecture. Research shows that at least 40 percent of our waking hours are spent listening. Within a few minutes following a discussion, the average listener is able to recall only 25 percent or less of what he heard. As the day goes on, even that percentage diminishes considerably.

In the corporate world, poor listening is responsible for the loss of billions of dollars due to unnecessary mistakes, lost opportunities, and minimal effectiveness. Faulty listening is often responsible for the letter that needs to be retyped time and again, the team that cannot produce results, or the physician who faces a malpractice suit. In our personal lives, low self-esteem, divorce, or family conflicts can be attributed to poor listening skills. If the need to listen better continues to be a recurrent theme in your work and home life, then this book is for you!

The mindful-listening approach is a mindset for connecting with people and information that stands up to the challenges of communicating in the twenty-first century. Look what you can gain:

- more fulfilling family, social, and professional relationships
- increased attention span
- better performance at interviews
- more cooperation from others
- improved productivity
- effective teamwork
- higher grades
- stronger knowledge base

- improved self-confidence
- better negotiation skills

Chances are, you have chosen this book because quick-fix attempts at achieving these personal and professional goals have been unsuccessful. Perhaps someone chose this book *for* you! Some of the students in my listening classes sign up, not because *their* listening skills are poor, but because they live or deal regularly with very poor listeners. The reasoning is, if these poor listeners won't change, maybe *they* can learn ways to get through to them. Even if only one party is at fault, both the poor listener *and* the speaker suffer, as do the managers *and* employees, husbands *and* wives, parents *and* children. In this book you will learn some ways in which you can be a good example for the other half. If indeed *you* are the one taking responsibility for improving a relationship by learning to enhance your listening skills, perhaps that incorrigible other may start to sense your desire to understand him better. Exercising fair listening encourages others to give us a turn at presenting our point of view. Often, by being better listeners ourselves, we can accomplish much more than by trying to change others.

Poor listening gets in the way of getting things done effectively. We are frantic to maximize our effectiveness in our daily must-do activities. It is important to spend time with our families, stay in shape, and be productive at work. But instead of achieving fulfillment through these endeavors, frequently just the opposite occurs. Many of us become disconnected from family, friends, and customers. The contradictions abound foremost in the workplace. Company downsizing has forced us to see our customers as mere statistics—a sales call, a medical procedure, a drop-in. "Customer satisfaction is our number one priority," says the boss, "but don't forget to keep the numbers up, be a team player, and maintain quality!" Reconciling these seemingly disparate demands is within your grasp!

It is by unleashing our powers of mindful listening that we can reconnect with others and be efficient as well. By changing our mindset toward listening, every interaction becomes a memorable one, each day an adventure. Best of all, by using our listening abilities to their fullest, we can set an example for others, particularly our children. Think about how much richer their lives will be if they learn the art of mindful listening when they're young. Many of us were conditioned to think that listening is a passive process, that it is the wiser person who does the talking.

Many learning specialists agree that a great number of children with learning disabilities have not been given adequate examples of good listening in the home. In 1995, the Carnegie Council on Adolescent Development completed a ten-year study that indicated that children are not getting enough interaction with parents or other adults. How can we expect our children to learn when we haven't taught them how to listen? The emphasis on computerized learning has been a boon to education in some respects. However, because of children's overexposure to fast-paced media (TV, video games, and computers) that reduce attention, listening, and concentration skills, educators are finding children more difficult to teach. One of the many challenges facing today's teachers is having to modify their teaching strategies to blend computer use with verbal interaction. Without a balanced approach, children may lose out on the development of interpersonal skills necessary to be successful in life. The personal interactions with teachers and other mentors throughout the years provide the groundwork for learning how to get along with adults other than our parents. In the classroom, students learn the give and take necessary to make and keep friends, how to successfully team up on projects—in short, *how to get along with others.* To allow technology to intrude upon that valuable education only furthers the growing trend of disconnectedness.

Growing up in the fifties and sixties, dinner-table talk was a staple activity in middle-class America. TV shows like *Father Knows Best* and *Leave It to Beaver* showed parents setting the stage for discussion about typical adolescent issues like peer pressures at school or jealousy between siblings. They showed children stating their feelings while parents listened with concern (they actually stopped eating!). The point was to illustrate how dinner-table discussions offered a family forum for character building. These forums addressed feelings and possible solutions—everyone participated. Of course, by the end of the program, everyone's problems were solved and all were happy again. The moral of these shows was to offer opportunities for caring discussion and put out the little fires before they get out of control.

Could schoolyard and family violence be mitigated by better listening? Researchers at the University of Minnesota and the University of North Carolina found that a parent's presence in the home at dinnertime was associated with a reduced incidence of drug use, sex, violence, and emotional distress among teens. Could we ever have imagined the Beaver getting to the point where he finds a gun and shoots Eddie for not giving him a ride in his new sports car?

Unlike most families on TV at that time, both my parents worked full time and all of my siblings were involved in extracurricular activities very much like families of today. My parents' friends would have labeled us a type-A family back in those days. Yet somehow my parents saw to it that every night the family sat down together for dinner for at least thirty minutes. Some of my family members came and went according to their schedules, but everybody got in on at least one topic of discussion or shared one event of the day with two or more family members. There, we developed our verbal and reasoning skills, learned how to argue a point, build ideas as a team, speak openly about our strengths and weaknesses, and listen. Now that we are all on our own, I believe that our lives were shaped by the magic that transpired around that table every night at six o'clock.

Many of us feel that if we do most of the talking, we will be perceived as knowledgeable and dynamic. Yet the communication situations we avoid are those in which one person, oblivious to the realities of others, does all the talking. A good listener is easy to spot—he is usually someone we look forward to talking with and being around. A good listener is not only one who processes the spoken word and the meaning behind the words accurately, but one who makes the speaker feel valued by encouraging him to expand on his ideas and feelings. A good listener touches the lives of those to whom he listens.

TV interviewers like Barbara Walters, Charlie Rose, Oprah Winfrey, and Larry King are examples of good listeners. It was said that Ernest Hemingway had a way of listening with such intensity that the person doing the speaking felt supremely complimented. Listening intently even for a minute is one of the nicest gifts we can give to another human being.

The lack of *self-listening* is often the cause of communication breakdown. If we could hear our words and comments through the ears of our listeners, we would be appalled at the overgeneralizations, the inaccuracies, and the insensitive, negative comments we make about ourselves and others. Learning to carefully select our words plays a major role in presenting ourselves in a favorable light, getting along well with others, and effectively getting the job done. When we make self-deprecating remarks about our looks, intelligence, or competence, we reveal an unhealthy mindset, chip away at our self-confidence, and create the wrong impressions, setting the stage for us not to be taken seriously.

We need to listen to ourselves to be sure we choose words that truly represent our meaning. Are our explanations concise and to the point? We may use words or a tone of voice that offend or turn people off to our message. These destructive communication behaviors push

18

the listener's limits and discourage hopes of future interaction. No wonder we become confused and annoyed with others when they don't respond according to our expectations. The listening mindset you are about to develop will also enable you to better tune into yourself and what motivates you to act the way you do.

Listening abilities are put to the test in adverse conditions. Stressful interactions may include asking for directions, a first date, or an important interview. The stress factor increases when we must deal with hostile customers or coworkers. Further escalation of emotions ensues with an overly assertive personality or a potentially violent one. When ideas and points of view collide, how well do we process the whole message without building up our defenses? A list of tricks will not assist us when listening under stress. Our success in these situations depends on the strength of our foundation as listeners—this includes breath control, ability to concentrate, and awareness of our barriers to listening and how we work with them, among other factors. Knowing how to listen well in less than optimal conditions is a valuable and necessary survival skill.

In order to reap the benefits of listening, we must let ourselves develop and expand our ability to concentrate. We should be able to sustain our focus for several minutes or as long as we choose, depending on the nature of the listening task. If the topic of conversation is light and familiar, concentration is much easier to sustain than if the material presented is dry and technical. Intent and interest in the subject matter also play a role in our willingness to concentrate. Stress, depression, and self-doubt have the potential to cripple our ability to attend to, much less concentrate on what someone is saying.

Many of my students in their forties or fifties take my listening course because they feel they are starting to lose their memories; they forget names, lose concentration, or miss details. Because of this concern, they are hesitant to take on new challenges like learning to use a computer or obtaining advanced degrees. In most cases, they are not on the verge of dementia. Rather, they have lost touch with the ability to focus for long periods of time. Other students wonder whether they have ADD (attention deficit disorder). These difficulties with concentration can affect our confidence for learning new tasks. The relationship between listening and memory is complex and beyond the scope of this book. However, a basic understanding of this relationship will better motivate us to apply some of the upcoming strategies.

Memory comprises three basic processes: encoding, storage, and retrieval. Encoding requires us to pay attention. During the encoding process, sensory information (words, pictures, music, etc.) is perceived. This information enters our *sensory memory*, where it is held for about one second. (Think of sensory memory as surface memory.) If we choose to further preserve this bit of information—directions to a new restaurant, for example—we need to take it to the next level of processing called *short-term memory* (STM). For the direction "left on Lehman and right on Hathaway" to enter STM, we need to repeat or rehearse it aloud to ourselves for about fifteen seconds. Our STM is able to hold on to plus or minus seven bits of information at a time, equal to the average phone number. If we want to retain these directions for use again in the future, we need to take this direction to a even deeper level of memory called *long-term memory* (LTM). There are various methods for the transfer of information to LTM. Drawing a map, picturing familiar landmarks (the Dunkin' Donuts will be on your right), or associating the street names with the names of familiar people, among other methods, can move those directions into long-term storage.

If we choose to *remember* or deeply process a phone number and put it in long-term memory, it may be necessary to make associations with other familiar numerical sequences. Do the four digits in a particular phone number (222-1812) remind us of an important year (the War of 1812), or is the pattern a visual one like 1-800-761-8008? Linking the memory of the interaction with the phone number is often helpful. If the discussion with this particular individual was a stormy one, then 1812 is a natural link. The process of associating new information with prior knowledge enables us to retrieve that information months or years later. We do not have to spend a lot of time to efficiently encode, store, and retrieve information (processing the directions to the restaurant from sensory memory to LTM took fewer than sixty seconds), but you must be able to concentrate.

Concentration is like a river. The stimulus or object of our attention may trickle into consciousness. Our interest heightens and other ideas (associations) enter our minds, similar to a stream fed by other streams. Unflustered by the obstacles in its path, the larger stream picks up strength and speed just as our enthusiasm hones our focus on the topic. As the stream becomes a river, the mind remains focused on the development of the thought or idea. That mental energy can be as powerful and sustaining as the undercurrent of a raging river. When someone speaks we can ignore the message, simply skim the surface, or follow the way of the river and concentrate.

The reality is that television, with its frequent commercial breaks, numerous choices (no thanks to the remote control), open-door policies, and our hectic, multifaceted lifestyles, has shortened our attention span and limited our opportunities for concentration. Fortunately, since most of our brains are still intact, it is possible to regain (or for many of us, uncover for the first time) the ability to focus our attention, concentrate, and restore confidence in our ability to learn.

I do not suggest that effective listening is a form of acting or a technique to be learned. On the contrary, we innately possess the ability to concentrate on verbal messages and deeply process information. Listening is one of our greatest personal natural resources, yet it is by far one of our most undeveloped abilities. Our education has emphasized speaking, reading, and writing, yet the activity that takes up a big hunk of our day—listening—is the one for which we receive the least training.

This book does not approach listening as a technique or group of skills to be learned. I even resist the phrase *active listening*. If we get hung up on a laundry list of listening to-dos, we can miss the speaker's message altogether. We do not need to manipulate our speakers by acting like we are listening, nor do we want to have to work at having a conversation. That is fake listening. Instead, let's take a look at what happens when our natural ability to listen catches us off guard.

Think of situations when you were particularly interested in a topic or when you were startled by an alarming news broadcast, say the Kennedy assassination or the events of September 11. Many of us can recall experiencing the tragic chill of being completely absorbed with the spoken words; we might even be able to recall where we were at the time or what we were doing. No skill set or technique came to mind as to how to listen—our inborn, *listening reflex* kicked in. But how can we achieve and maintain a similar level of absorption during everyday conversation, at a lecture, or during a heated discussion?

To accomplish this does not require extensive course work. It does require a change in our mindset toward listening. It begins by opening our minds to accept the notion that any verbal encounter could contain a golden nugget of experience, information, or insight, quite often when we least expect it.

Sometimes, the greatest insight of my day comes from the person who cleans my office. The commitment to a change in attitude or mindset toward listening allows our innate listening abilities to kick in. This leads to a change in behavior. People's positive reactions toward us and our improved efficiency will perpetuate our new listening outlook!

Mindful listening is presented here as a synergy of three factors—*relaxation, focus,* and a *desire to learn* or gain another's perspective. This mindset involves becoming aware of the barriers we have built toward others, our inner obstacles, and how to put them aside. For every tiny change we make each day in our listening the rewards are tenfold. My students report feeling more positive about themselves and their relationships. They notice how their business interactions are more successful, and they feel more fulfilled at day's end.

Most of the ideas expressed in this book have roots in Eastern philosophy and Zen Buddhism, yet they are not intended to convey or conflict with any religious point of view, nor are these approaches mystical or occult. Contrary to what some people think about Zen and Buddhism—that these concepts are strictly contemplative and intellectual—the philosophy and mindset presented in this book are very practical and easily understood. The Zen Buddhist philosophy gives us ways of dealing with everyday challenges. It teaches us how focus, concentration, and compassion keep our everyday lives healthy, peaceful, and productive. Zen is a process of undoing rote behaviors rather than learning new ones. Zen helps to dissolve the habits destructive to effective communication—prejudice, negativism, closed-mindedness, and preoccupation with the self—and cultivate their opposites. I do not profess to be an expert in Eastern thought, nor have I attained enlightenment. Nevertheless, what I have studied and applied assists me with many of life's challenges. Listening effectively is one of those challenges. My students, patients, and I have found that these simple concepts have the power to transform the average listening situation into an opportunity for self-development and relationship building.

We may look at Zen Buddhism as a psychology or philosophy about life. Listening with the heart, body, and mind requires a change in our attitude toward how we relate to the speaker. It involves focusing on the *process* of listening versus the *payoff.* The Zen approach to listening offers us insight into our true nature, or *kensho*. This heightened awareness frees us from the confinement of self-interest and self-consciousness that bars us from connecting with the minds of others.

The origins of Zen Buddhism go back about twenty-five hundred years to northern India, when Gautama Siddhartha, a humble prince, left his cushy life to better understand the nature of existence. He lived like a beggar and watched the suffering brought on by old age, famine, and loneliness. After meditating for six years, he became enlightened to the truth of existence and became known as the Buddha—the Awakened One. Buddhism took two directions after the death of Gautama Buddha, the Theravada tradition that spread to southwest Asia, and the Mahayana tradition that mingled with Taoism in China and then spread to Japan where it was called Zen. The Mahayana way emphasized spiritual development and meditation as the vehicle to awakening to the true reality of life. Both branches of Buddhism share many of the same beliefs, but Zen Buddhism is known for its simple and straightforward application to everyday life. Gautama Buddha realized that discontent in life is the result of attachment to things and the way we think things should be. Nonsentient, or unenlightened human beings (most of us, that is) are distracted to the point of being deluded by egocentric thinking, self-consciousness, yearning for what we don't have, and wishing we were somewhere else. The torment in our lives is brought about by working so hard to be separate from everyone else. Therefore, we continually grasp for status, material possessions, speed, and extraneous preoccupations to be one up against the competition—our neighbors. These attempts to work against ourselves and others serve only to bring on more distress in the form of anxiety, illness, depression, and other more serious tragedies in our society.

These are exactly the reasons why poor listeners make life so much more difficult for themselves. They crave attention as the speaker, think about what to say next while others are still talking, interrupt to take control of the conversation, hold fast to opinions, constantly dwell on the past or dream about the future, and other self-defeating behaviors. The purpose of *The Zen of Listening* is to help you reverse these trends so as to make your life and the lives of those around you more satisfying and effective. Also, by exercising mindful listening a little bit every day, others will start to respond to you more favorably, even difficult people.

The distractions and human concerns of the twenty-first century require mindful listening more than ever before. If we want to put an end to prejudice, racism, conflict, and suffering it won't happen with a just-do-it attitude or an active-listening approach. As long as we think about trying to listen, we will not be able to hear clearly. Altering our mental foundation for better listening must come first. It is like giving a beggar a cookbook and saying, "Here, enjoy your meal!" He has no heat, no pots and pans, no cooking skills, just the will to eat but little means to accomplish it. He might also lack the vigilance and patience to cook the food correctly. However, once he is given the basic necessities, sees the value in being able to cook, and gets some practice at it, the cookbook will serve him well. Eventually he will be able to cook without the book, as long as he cooks a little bit every day. Despite the fact that many of the listening discoveries that I describe in this book are derived from my experience as a speech therapist in a medical setting, they have universal application. The methods I propose have been tried and tested not only by hundreds of my workshop participants in the last few years, but for centuries by scientists, Zen masters, and their students. Over 90 percent of my students have found at least one of the strategies for attaining mindful listening key to making their lives happier and more productive. The success of mindful listening is due to its simplicity and applicability to everyday life.

Just as each reader sees life from a different angle, different approaches to mindful listening are presented here. We all have different listening needs and concerns. Some of us take classes or read books about listening in hopes of improving our interpersonal or marital relationships; others, because we want to do better in school. Some of us seek new careers or look for ways to improve ourselves or make happier customers. Therefore, I have approached the subject of listening from a few different angles. One main theme supports them all: the best listeners see listening as a process rather than a goal.

You may find a few chapters key to your ability to listen better, or you may need to spend more time on the reflection and relaxation sections before you can apply some of the other ideas. Read through each chapter thoughtfully. Once you have digested these thoughts, take a few days or weeks to apply the exercises at the end of each chapter. The rewards of good listening will happen without working for them. Judging from the comments and letters I have received from former students, this approach to listening has been very helpful.

Make your new behaviors habits by using the buddy system or creating visual reminders in your home or office. Once you have established a new awareness in your daily routine, notice how you become more attentive to people and things. Move on to the next chapter and incorporate another step. At the end of each day reflect for a few moments on how well you did, how differently and positively people responded to you, or how much more information you were able to recall.

Using this cumulative approach of reflection and application, you will, by the time you are finished with this book, have abandoned any narrow and self-limiting views about listening. You will be free to experience the vast richness of each person you meet and be able to absorb the wealth of knowledge and opportunity that exists with every waking breath.

How Well Are You Listening Now?

Why not go out on a limb?
That's where the fruit is.

—Will Rogers

*H*ow tiresome it is to leave a performance review with the comment written in bold print: **"Your listening skills need work."** It is a déjà vu experience for many of us, one that we can easily recall from numerous early sources: our parents, scout leaders, coaches, and teachers. Since our youth these words of wisdom have come in various forms. For example: "Stop talking and pay attention," as if when we stop talking we somehow start paying attention, or more indirectly, "Maybe you should get your hearing checked." When we are told to listen up, what exactly does that mean? How do we know if we are really listening (and paying attention) or just acting like we are? How can we convince others, like the boss, that our listening skills are deserving of a promotion? Would we know a good listener if we met one? How far are we from being considered a good listener?

Self-knowledge is the first step toward self-improvement. Let's take a look at how well you listen today. This pretest will also make you aware of the wide spectrum of listening behaviors we intend to discuss. Carefully consider each question and indicate whether or not you consistently demonstrate each behavior. Then check your responses with the answer key on the next page and total your score.

Do you:

1. Think about what *you* are going to say while the speaker is talking?
❑ Yes, consistently ❑ No, almost never ❑ Sometimes

2. Tune out people who say things you don't agree with or don't want to hear?
❑ Yes, consistently ❑ No, almost never ❑ Sometimes

3. Learn something from each person you meet, even if it is ever so slight?
❑ Yes, consistently ❑ No, almost never ❑ Sometimes

4. Keep eye contact with the person who is speaking?
❑ Yes, consistently ❑ No, almost never ❑ Sometimes

5. Become self-conscious in one-to-one or small group conversations?
❑ Yes, consistently ❑ No, almost never ❑ Sometimes

6. Often interrupt the speaker?
❑ Yes, consistently ❑ No, almost never ❑ Sometimes

7. Fall asleep or daydream during meetings or presentations?
❑ Yes, consistently ❑ No, almost never ❑ Sometimes

8. Restate instructions or messages to be sure you understood correctly?
❑ Yes, consistently ❑ No, almost never ❑ Sometimes

9. Allow the speaker to vent negative feelings towards you without becoming defensive or physically tense?
❑ Yes, consistently ❑ No, almost never ❑ Sometimes

10. Listen for the meaning behind the speaker's words through gestures and facial expressions?
❑ Yes, consistently ❑ No, almost never ❑ Sometimes

11. Feel frustrated or impatient when communicating with persons from other cultures?
❑ Yes, consistently ❑ No, almost never ❑ Sometimes

12. Inquire about the meaning of unfamiliar words or jargon?
❑ Yes, consistently ❑ No, almost never ❑ Sometimes

13. Give the appearance of listening when you are not?
❑ Yes, consistently ❑ No, almost never ❑ Sometimes

14. Listen to the speaker without judging or criticizing ?
❑ Yes, consistently ❑ No, almost never ❑ Sometimes

15. Start giving advice before you are asked?
❏ Yes, consistently ❏ No, almost never ❏ Sometimes

16. Ramble on before getting to the point?
❏ Yes, consistently ❏ No, almost never ❏ Sometimes

17. Take notes when necessary to help you remember?
❏ Yes, consistently ❏ No, almost never ❏ Sometimes

18. Consider the state of the person you are talking to (nervous, rushed, hearing impaired, etc.)?
❏ Yes, consistently ❏ No, almost never ❏ Sometimes

19. Let a speaker's physical appearance or mannerisms distract you from listening?
❏ Yes, consistently ❏ No, almost never ❏ Sometimes

20. Remember a person's name after you have been introduced?
❏ Yes, consistently ❏ No, almost never ❏ Sometimes

21. Assume you know what the speaker is going to say and stop listening?
❏ Yes, consistently ❏ No, almost never ❏ Sometimes

22. Feel uncomfortable allowing silence between you and your conversation partner?
❏ Yes, consistently ❏ No, almost never ❏ Sometimes

23. Ask for feedback to make sure you are getting across to the other person?
❏ Yes, consistently ❏ No, almost never ❏ Sometimes

24. Preface your statements with unflattering remarks about yourself?
❏ Yes, consistently ❏ No, almost never ❏ Sometimes

25. Think more about building warm working relationships with team members and customers than about bringing in revenue?
❏ Yes, consistently ❏ No, almost never ❏ Sometimes

SCORING: Compare your answers with those on the chart below. For every answer that matches the key, give yourself one point. If you answered "Sometimes" to any of the questions, score half a point. Total the number of points.

1	N	6	N	11	N	16	N	21	N
2	N	7	N	12	Y	17	Y	22	N
3	Y	8	Y	13	N	18	Y	23	Y
4	Y	9	Y	14	Y	19	N	24	N
5	N	10	Y	15	N	20	Y	25	Y

Total points: _____

If you scored twenty-one or more points, congratulations! Continue to read on and reinforce what you already are doing well. Note which areas could use further improvement. Are there any listening behaviors that require more consistency? Chapters four, six, and nine will be particularly helpful in strengthening your listening ability. Good listeners can fine-tune listening under stress (chapter nine) and help others listen better.

A score of sixteen to twenty suggests that you usually absorb most of the main ideas, but often miss a good portion of the rest of the message due to difficulties with sustaining attention. You may feel detached from the speaker and start thinking about other things or about what you are going to say next. Students who score at this level frequently comment that rechecking details is often needed. Chapters six and ten will be particularly helpful in this regard. Examine typical response styles (chapter seven) that may prevent you from receiving that extra information.

If you scored between ten and fifteen points, you may be focusing more on your own agenda than the speaker's needs. You easily become distracted and perceive listening as a task. Perhaps personal biases get in the way of fully understanding the speaker. Chapter four will help you work through many of the obstacles that prevent you from receiving the whole message. Pay special attention to chapters five and six, which set the foundation for sustaining your focus on the spoken message. If you find it particularly difficult to process spoken information in stressful listening situations, a few basics from the earlier chapters will help you benefit from the information in chapter nine.

Those of you who scored fewer than nine points will notice the most dramatic improvement in your communication by applying the suggestions given in this book. Most of the time you experience listening as a boring activity. You might complain often that your memory is poor and feel great frustration when trying to retain information from presentations and succeed in a classroom situation.

If you answered "Sometimes" to many of the questions, then obviously you are a sometimes listener. Chances are your ability to concentrate may be at fault and/or you are a highly critical individual and quick to judge whether a listening opportunity is worthwhile. However, there have been times when you have experienced the satisfaction of being fully absorbed in what someone has to say. Imagine how successful and effective you could be if you would let yourself experience that sense of total absorption in every listening opportunity.

Now that we have a taste of some of the ingredients for good listening, let's come up with a good working definition. If you were to poll various individuals and ask what it means to be a good listener, you would hear several versions. Here are some examples. Sales consultant Michael Leppo describes good listening as the ability to hear attentively. Michelle Lucas, a psychotherapist, says that good listening is a process of showing respect and validating a person's worth. The International Listening Association defines listening as "the process of receiving, constructing meaning from, and responding to spoken and/or nonverbal messages." Others say it is simply the ability to understand and remember what was said. Ralph G. Nichols, one of the founding fathers of listening studies, said, "Listening is an inside job—inside action on the part of the listener." This suggests that good listening is the ability to get into the shoes of the speaker in order to see his side of the issue.

As you can see, a practical definition of listening must take into account its many aspects. For the purpose of this book, I will define a good listener as one who is *mindful* of the wide spectrum of listening skills. These include the ability to

- receive the spoken word accurately, interpret the whole message (the words, gestures and facial expressions) in an unbiased manner;

- retain the information for future use;

- sustain attention to the spoken word at will; listening is a process that occurs *over time;*

- attend to *your* speech and be sensitive to the accuracy of the message and the possible interpretations that could be derived from it;

- encourage a speaker to speak from his heart and expound on his or her ideas without censure. This makes your speaker feel valued and respected.

This book teaches you that the real power in communication lies in using your natural ability to listen: to process information, gain insight, and retain information so you can put it to work. Mindful listening is already a part of you. However, it does require a desire to listen. A desire to listen involves a curiosity for new information and a willingness to pay more respect to your speaker. If your desire is to build stronger personal and professional relationships, a degree of compassion is a basic requirement to becoming a better listener.

Mindful listening is the mind and body working together to communicate. Furthermore, it does not require two functioning ears to listen in a mindful way. Mindful listening requires you to see, hear, and feel with your whole being. To attend mindfully to the message, whether the message is spoken or signed, is to perceive as closely as possible the intent and experience of the speaker.

Mindful listening can be applied to the wide continuum of listening types:

- information processing

- information seeking

- critical or evaluative listening

- therapeutic listening

- empathetic or compassionate listening

- small-talk listening

In any given situation there is much overlap between the various kinds of listening. For example, when meeting someone for the first time, small talk may spark a discussion about a shared topic of interest. That may lead one of the partners to relate some controversial information learned on the Internet. The listener may have doubts about the information based on her prior knowledge; a friendly debate on that topic could ensue. Various other combinations may occur depending upon whether the discussion takes place in a classroom, a service center, a bus stop, or a party. In all of these settings, mindful listening is effective.

Now that we have surveyed the vast landscape of good listening, let's begin our journey through the brush and start clearing a path towards realizing our listening goals.

Awakening Your Sense of Listening

Toto, I don't think we're in Kansas anymore.
      —Dorothy, *The Wizard of Oz*

Most of us with good hearing cannot imagine a world of silence, just as those of us with the ability to taste cannot imagine a life of not tasting. Unfortunately, it is when we lose these precious gifts that we realize how we took them for granted. If lost and then found, we savor their presence like never before.

A photo album, thought long gone, reappears beneath a pile of baby clothes and thirty-year-old toys. The sweet-sick smell of slightly molding leather and paper rises as you lift it reverently from its forgotten spot. You open the cover and gaze at the faces looking back at you. Feelings of joy and melancholy make you ache a bit all over. The sticky, dusty edges of the photos catch on your fingers as you turn the pages. Would you have treated that album with the same respect and appreciation if it had been kept on your coffee table day after day? Probably not.

Hearing is the sense that allows you to listen to your world. It is the sense that perceives and discriminates between sounds. Listening is the process of making sense out of these signals and translating them into meaning. The gift of hearing and our magnificent ability to listen are often taken for granted. Our lives change considerably when we develop a hearing problem or lose our acuity for the sound of a bird or a whisper.

A hearing problem can be due to wax, fluid, or infection. It can be noise or drug induced, accompanied by age or damage to the auditory nerves. In many cases it can be treated or assisted. These impediments to listening are often not under our control; they are a function of age or environment. Sometimes this vast array of sounds bombarding our ears is so complex that, in order for us to survive this information overload, we need to exert some control over what we listen to. Listening predicaments arise when

- your self-interest keeps some voices permanently in the background when they should be in the foreground, or

- your attention is so scattered that you have a hard time keeping selected information in the foreground.

Later in the book we will address these listening problems that stem from self-imposed filtering and poor concentration. But before we tackle the problems, let's take a few minutes to explore the wonders of our hearing and listening abilities.

Begin by closing your eyes wherever you are right now. Listen to the different sounds around you. Notice how the textures of the sounds vary. Hear the whir of the overhead fan as it resists the air. Contrast that with the featherlike flutter of a gentle breeze outside your window. Now count the sounds you can perceive all at once—for instance, the ticking of the clock, the car turning the corner, the sound of pouring coffee, and many others.

Do you hear how some sounds are fainter or louder than others? Marvel at your ability to direct your attention to one sound and shift to another at will, remaining well aware of the sounds you have left behind. You have names for all these sounds and have experienced them at different levels. You've tasted some, ridden in others, held some in your hand. Many of these sounds you have judged and categorized according to their desirability. It is a wonder how these sounds have worked their way into your consciousness.

Right now I am sitting in front of my computer, and I can hear several layers of sound around me. If I take a minute to pay attention to this little symphony, it is interesting to note that, while a small part of my brain is processing this auditory information, it is also reminding me that it is about seven-thirty on a Saturday night. I hear the dishwasher on the rinse cycle (the rinse cycle is a higher pitch than the wash cycle). Someone is watching CNN in the living room (the news anchor's voice is very familiar to me), and my dog, Spud, is snoring at my feet in concert with the steady hum emanating from my computer. Occasionally a car drives down the street or the phone rings and interrupts these steady rhythms. If an unusual noise, however soft, would creep into this mosaic of sound, I would question it immediately. A gentle tinkling of the chandelier or a whisper through my window would stand out like an alarm and claim my attention.

All sounds, no matter what their source, are vibrations at various pitches. The vibrations are gathered by the outer ear (those odd-shaped receptacles on either side of our heads) and travel into the middle ear where the sound waves cause the eardrum to vibrate. That in turn causes the three tiny bones in the inner ear, called *ossicles*, to vibrate. The quality, loudness, volume, and resonance differentiate one set of vibrations from another. The light raining sound of my dishwasher contrasts substantially with the wider range of pitches and timbre flowing from my dog's nostrils.

The vibrations move from the middle ear through the snail-shaped, fluid-filled inner ear called the *cochlea*. The microscopic hair cells in the cochlea convert the fluid movement into electrical energy. This energy is transmitted by the hair cells to the hearing or *auditory nerve*. The auditory nerve automatically sends electrical signals to our brains to let us know that a woman versus a man is speaking on TV right now. Women's voices tend to lie within a pitch range of 139 to 1108 Hz while men's voice have a pitch range between 78 and 698 Hz. From the vast catalogue of female characters logged in our memory banks, we can discern which woman is talking by the degree of nasality in her voice, any accent that may be present, and the rhythm and inflection of her words. We can determine the emotion behind the words based on volume, pitch, and rate of speech. We know whether we like her or find her worth listening to.

The words themselves—stock prices, political analyses, sports scores—supply information, but primarily serve to reinforce our hunches about who's talking based on voice characteristics alone. Simultaneously, the brain is also receiving sounds from the dog, the dishwasher, and the street without causing mass confusion, only calm acceptance that, yes, this is a typical Saturday night.

A patient at the clinic, Jane Sokol Shulman, gradually began losing her hearing in elementary school. At age seventeen, she started to notice difficulty hearing the fine differences between speech sounds. Over the next two decades, Jane lost more and more of her hearing. Despite excellent lip-reading skills, she had become dependent on hearing aids while completing her education. By age thirty-seven, Jane could no longer use a telephone, even with the most powerful amplification. At that point, she accepted her deafness and eventually became president of the Boston chapter of the Association of Late-Deafened Adults (ALDA).

Even though Jane had accepted her new life, she still longed for the world of sound. She had learned about a surgical procedure called a cochlear implant and began researching the possibility of restoring some of her hearing. Jane had learned about the mixed results among other latent-deaf persons and was aware of the possibly rigorous rehabilitation period that would follow implantation of the device. But lip-reading was exhausting and it limited her job options. The sense of isolation and exclusion among her hearing friends had become intolerable. In 1997, Jane decided to have the implant procedure.

A few weeks after her surgery I had the opportunity to sit in on one of her rehabilitation sessions. Listening to Jane describe the awakening of her hearing ability had me nailed to my seat. Jane goes on to tell her story:

> So what is it like to hear again? The first word that comes to mind is *weird* and the second one is *miraculous*. . . . The biggest surprise was my auditory acuity. Nothing had prepared me for the shock of hearing soft sounds. Knowing that I could hear footsteps behind me and the chime when I leave my headlights on made me feel safer and more secure. Birds chirping, rain, rustling papers— I became reacquainted with the subliminal sounds that anchor us in the environment. I discovered new sounds, such as the beeps of ATM keys. And I rediscovered how supremely annoying other sounds are, such as laugh tracks on television. . . . I constantly found myself wishing I could focus on developing my new hearing without also having to manage my job, family, and household responsibilities as well. The amazement and wonder were overwhelming at times. I could hear people behind me saying "excuse me." Casual chitchat with strangers was no longer a Herculean effort. I could once again participate in these nonevents that hearing people take for granted, the social glue that holds us together.

A few times over the next several days, try this listening exercise. Even if you are not a music lover, try to listen objectively. Find a concert on the radio and see if you can pick out the different voices, instruments, and harmonies. Try isolating one particular voice or instrument for as many seconds as possible. Then return your attention to the blending of all the instruments and take in the whole piece. Notice how each voice is necessary to carry this performance, but that each voice alone is just a fragment of the whole. Now, without analyzing or dissecting the musical performance, sit for a few minutes and take in the music. Simply be witness to it. When we listen to music in this way, we get a taste of the Zen approach to listening. You are not thinking about the notes that came before the ones you are listening to now, nor are you anticipating the next passage. You are not judging the piece nor worrying about how long it is. You are just absorbing the music with your whole being as the music moves and changes. This is the interval of mental space that needs to be present when listening to another human being. To widen the gap of time between perceiving a message and interpreting its content is the essence of mindful listening.

In Chinese, characters or pictograms communicate ideas and situations. The character for *listening attentively* consists of the characters for Ear, Standing Still, Ten, Eye, and Heart and Mind. According to Zen Master Dae Gak, this pictogram for listening attentively means, "When in stillness, one listens with the heart. The ear is worth ten eyes." When we listen for the whole message, our senses need to be poised and focused, like a deer that freezes its gaze in the direction of a lurking predator.

Wherever you are, listen to how sounds, great and barely perceivable, come from all directions. At all times, a 360-degree vista of sound fills our ears. Ping-pong in the basement, steam from the iron, Bach down the hall, and the sweeping sound of the rowing machine upstairs makes us feel as if we are in a constant bubble of sound. Many noises bring out feelings and emotions more than words. The rustle of falling leaves and birds chirping in the woods spark thoughts about the seasons. The sound of waves is mesmerizing and soothes an unquiet mind. For decades, sounds and their effects on us have been the object of scientific research for the purposes of treating stress-related disorders. It is the process of listening over time to the sound of the loons on a lake or a spring rain that gradually calms our minds. It is not an instantaneous effect, nor would we want those sounds to be fleeting. We prefer to luxuriate for minutes and hours in the call of the seagulls or the pop and sizzle of a crackling hearth. Some say that we can become smarter listening to Mozart.

Even a single sound can release a flood of thoughts and sensations held captive in our memory's lost-and-found. The sound of a marching band in the distance reminds us of the football games and parades we experienced while growing up. The rush of a train overhead recalls commuting to the city for our first job. We all have moments when sound takes us back to another time and place.

Almost against my will, a familiar song from the sixties will sweep me back in time to my school cafeteria along with the mouth-watering smell of the chocolate chip cookies famous at Homewood-Flossmoor high school. The tune of "Hey, Jude" by the Beatles, a frequently played selection on the jukebox around lunch time, is accompanied by feelings of hunger and exhaustion after emerging from gym class across the hall. How strange and powerful is our sense of hearing to be able to transfer our consciousness at lightning speed to another time and place.

Indeed, some sounds are more pleasant than others. But these less melodious noises, like a smoke alarm or a jackhammer, connect with our survival or quality of life. Despite their unpleasing characteristics we are grateful for what they represent, in this case, preventing a fire and mending a broken water main. They draw our attention to issues concerning our well-being. In fact, many sounds are so necessary to our existence that despite their pleasant or unpleasant qualities, we accept them unconditionally. All sounds play a role in balancing our environment; each sound plays a role in the big picture. Can you imagine having equal tolerance for listening to your best friend tell about her new job and your most agitated customer complaining about his late order?

Yet to attend to every sound equally would be chaotic and possibly life-threatening. In our information-rich society the ability to tune into selected auditory information and sustain our attention to it while tuning out background noise is becoming more of a challenge. When we spread our listening too thin, we run the risk of making hasty decisions based on processing only bits and pieces of major issues. On the other hand, if we are too selective with the people or the programs we listen to, we run the risk of becoming so judgmental and critical that we become closed-minded. The goal in listening is to find the balance between focusing our attention and remaining open-minded and tolerant of different views.

The most negative and sometimes heartless forces working against our good intentions to strike that balance are our *mental barriers*. Let's continue along our course of self-discovery to prepare for a close encounter with the enemy.

The Great Walls of Misunderstanding

May we open to a deeper understanding
And a genuine love and caring
For the multitude of faces
Who are none other than ourself.

—Wendy Egyoku Nakao

*B*arriers are the distractions, prejudices, judgment calls, and preconceived notions about a person and the value of his message. Zen Masters refer to these barriers as *unwholesome mental formations, mental obscurations,* and *ignorance.* They believe that the people who are most unhappy in this world are those with irrational perceptions of people and ideas. Many of us think that the more toys, stocks, and houses we accumulate, the happier and more serene we will be. Some of us strive to identify with prestigious people and hang out at the right clubs in hope that some of that prestige will rub off on us and make us feel better about ourselves. We can be deluded into thinking that if we lose what we have, we'll be miserable. In terms of listening, such delusional thinking can block new ideas—

ideas with the potential for creativity and innovation. We can be frightened by what looks like a snake in the water, only to find upon closer inspection that it is just a piece of rope resting in a puddle. These perceptions are not just the product of our collective consciousness passed down through the generations; we manage to add our own special twist to further contort the perception. Instead of just an ordinary snake in the water, we now see a deadly viper.

To see into our own nature, to become aware of the barriers we create between ourselves and others, is the first step in creating a mindset conducive to becoming a good listener. Awareness of our actions, noting our programmed tendencies to unfairly judge others, is the goal of Zen.

These barriers may take the form of filters that allow only selected words and ideas into our consciousness and screen out the less familiar and uncomfortable messages. Therefore, only *pieces* of the message are received—the comfortable pieces that fit our stereotypes. Clinging to unsubstantiated biases and misperceptions brings pain and unhappiness to our lives. It is not so much the barriers themselves that create communication disasters but the emotions associated with them—jealousy, hatred, and desire. Moreover, like weeds in a garden, these barriers choke our potential for developing fruitful relationships and fresh ideas. The good news is that you can escape these great walls—if you choose.

As an example, let's create a fictitious group of people toward whom you are prejudiced. Let's say they come from a country called Batamia. Imagine that you grew up in a Batamian neighborhood and accumulated a wealth of information about Batamians. Your family, of strictly Losmanian ancestry, always disliked Batamians. In fact, your parents pointed out aspects of Batamian women's personalities that you never even noticed before. You got to be such an expert at disliking Batamian women that you started to notice even more undesirable traits as these women began to appear in your workplace.

Even though you may have had a few pleasant Batamian neighbors, they were the minority. Now your dislike is so well honed that you have developed a dislike for anyone who even *looks* Batamian. Your recollection of the women in your neighborhood is, among other things, that they are lazy and complain a lot. Therefore, when Mrs. Jones, a Batamian woman in your office, complains about the lack of adequate support staff, you simply disregard her comment. It is easy for you to brush her off and close your mind to her very real problem. However, if a male coworker, someone who easily intimidates you, makes the same complaint and you act on it, you may find yourself penalized by your own barriers in the form of a sex discrimination suit. Barriers, at the very least, can cost money, reputations, and careers.

Some barriers are so impenetrable that they may totally restrict certain persons from entering our ear space. If you are fervently religious or totally committed to a cause, you may be unwilling to give any serious attention to the views of someone with different beliefs. Let's ask ourselves: Why shut our ears to this new information? Is a different take on a topic something to be feared? Is it unsettling to think that a different viewpoint might force us to change the way we think? Does our ability to say no evaporate if we give someone a few minutes to describe his point of view?

If you are a negative thinker to begin with, you may fear change because it can disrupt the status quo. Your boss and your marriage partner may not agree, your friends might leave you. If you see the cup as half full, however, change could mean a more challenging job, a more compatible spouse, or friends who are supportive instead of competitive. These blocks to listening can stifle our creativity and limit our knowledge base. In addition, they can become so obtrusive that they affect our ability to pay attention and concentrate.

If we look at all the listening opportunities that present themselves, they generally fall into two categories—events (shows, lectures) and people. People fall into further categories: those we want to listen to and those we don't—even if we know we should. When we *want* to listen, there are few obstacles to receiving the message. We easily welcome good music, a funny joke, or a discussion on our favorite hobby. It serves us well also to *want* to listen to what we *should* listen to—a loved one or a lecture we signed up for. If we choose not to listen to someone or something, we may have some very good reasons for that. Perhaps their voice hurts our ears, the message is offensive or of no interest. Our barriers become clearer to us when we feel we *should* listen to someone or something that we *don't* want to listen to: a disgruntled employee, our teenager's plea for a new wardrobe, our company's new quality-assurance standards. However, there may be unpleasant consequences for not listening in these situations. If we cannot disregard the consequences, then we have to listen.

What are the obstacles that keep us from getting the whole message in these should-listen activities, and why can't we let ourselves accept a differing point of view? Barriers that appear very logical to us may prevent us from being receptive to what our speaker has to say. If you are having marital problems, why, for heaven's sake, would you listen to the advice of a counselor who is a recovered alcoholic and twice married? Before heading for the nearest exit, though, take a moment to consider: Maybe he's got more common sense about relationships than someone who stays in an abusive marriage. Did his rehabilitation give him more insight into working through problems than someone who never had to overcome an addiction? Maybe he lost his spouse to unfortunate circumstances beyond his control? Perhaps you'll give him a chance after all.

Getting through the fog of distractions and personal biases to allow the message to be heard is a challenge to the listener. When we are aware of our obstacles, we are then better able to deal with them. We may not be able to eliminate these barriers—many of them were programmed into our psyches in childhood. However, if we face our barriers and witness their pervasive power to shut out opportunities for personal growth, we can allow them to be more transparent. After that point, we can get on with the business of listening. Some of the great walls that prevent us from getting the full message include:

- background noise

- status

- gender, race, and age prejudice

- physical appearance

- past experiences

- personal agendas

- focusing on the outcome versus the process of listening

- negative self-talk

Many of these obstacles to better listening are learned from our parents, our culture, and the media. They begin as preferences (what do we like better, apples or oranges?) and evolve to steadfast points of view.

It is only human to have preferences and opinions. The difficulty begins when we feel compelled to defend our opinions and ignore evidence to the contrary. This leads to argumentative and aggressive behavior. According to Voltaire, "Opinion has caused more trouble in this earth than all the plagues and earthquakes."

Some of our barriers are the product of minibrainwashings that have now become our reality. These biases learned from TV, movies, and our parents seep into the subconscious and create much needless suffering. For example, most of us dread Monday morning because of its bad reputation. We've worked hard to perpetuate that reputation by using our Sunday nights to agonize over our most undesirable work tasks and dream up disastrous circumstances that could make Monday miserable. Monday arrives and we almost reflexively moan at the sound of the alarm and snap at the driver who took our parking space. Mondays have become problem days because we see to it on a regular basis that the prophecy is fulfilled. These delusions are all learned and selectively programmed biases in our minds. The truth may be that Monday is no different than another day; as a matter of fact, we're rested after a weekend, and on Wednesday or Thursday we've probably met with different but equally daunting challenges. The only difference is that we haven't inherited or developed a distorted mindset for Wednesday or Thursday.

Fortunately, the fact that we enjoy certain preferences does not mean that we have to despise their alternatives. Our hands are a good example. We may be right-handed, yet we do not ignore or reject our left hand because we don't use it to write, swing a tennis racket, or hammer a nail. For most activities, in fact, we need both hands. When I feel that a certain preference is overtaking my ability to listen, I think of my hands and how I depend on both of them to get me through my day. We need to develop the same ambidexterity when it comes to listening.

Dr. Marshall Rosenberg, in his book *Nonviolent Communication,* tells how we find it difficult to separate *observation* of a situation, person, or thing from an *evaluation.* Rosenberg calls our tendencies to observe and judge at the same time "life-alienating communication."

For example, when we start listening to someone talk about the economy, we immediately observe her looks, mannerisms, voice, sex, and age, and sift these observations through our personal filters. After only seconds we have judged whether she is worth listening to (the chances of continuing to listen are much greater, by the way, if her opinions agree with ours). Can you imagine what it would be like to just listen to someone without jumping to judge or evaluate? According to Indian philosopher J. Krishnamurti, "To observe without evaluating is the highest form of intelligence."

We may not be able to rid ourselves entirely of these great walls, but we can get a better understanding of why we don't connect with certain individuals and why some persons have trouble connecting with us. Furthermore, mental barriers interfere with our ability to be flexible in our thinking. The ability to accept change and adapt to change either at home or the workplace is directly related to our ability to be flexible with different ways of seeing the world. Some of these walls will yield more easily than others. As you go through the list on page 49, start by thinking about the people you don't want to listen to, but *should* listen to. Try to identify the obstacles that are your most frequent barriers to listening.

First consider the obvious. How can we expect to "mind-meld," as Mr. Spock would say, with our speaker if the TV or radio is too loud or if the office is full of **background noise**? We generally speak at a volume level of about sixty to seventy decibels. Office noise—people talking in the next cubicle, the rustle of papers, the hum of equipment—can compete with and exceed those volume levels, masking the speaker's voice. We know how difficult it is to have decent conversation at a noisy bar or a wedding reception where everyone ends up screaming across the table just to be heard over the band. One of the simplest courtesies we can extend to our speaker is to eliminate these distractions. If we want to have a meaningful conversation in these situations, go to a quieter place or eliminate the noise source. Even though we have two ears we can listen to only one thing at a time.

By the way, how is your hearing? The American Speech and Hearing Association estimates that over thirty million people in this country have a hearing loss that could be treated. A great way to discourage others from sharing information with you is to ignore a perceptual hearing problem that could be improved with wax removal, a hearing aid, or an assistive listening device (ALD). Hearing aids cannot restore hearing, but they can maximize whatever hearing capacity is still present. Approximately six million Americans wear hearing aids. Seven to eight million people would benefit from them but are not wearing them. Technological advances in hearing aids (digital hearing aids) in the last few years provide better sound quality than ever before. Many others would be helped by ALDs, such as phone adapters, speech amplifiers, FM systems in movie theaters, TV closed-captioning, and various alerting devices. Lip-reading courses, generally taught by audiologists or speech pathologists, are another option to enhancing one-to-one communication.

Many children and adults with acquired nerve deafness can benefit from cochlear implants. As I mentioned earlier in Jane's story, it is a surgically implanted device with an externally worn speech processor that stimulates the surviving auditory fibers in the inner ear. Although there are risks to consider (as in any surgical procedure), cochlear implant is recognized by the American Medical Association as standard treatment for profound hearing loss.

Ringing in the ears and head noises, or *tinnitus,* is believed to be brought on by noise and stress. Persons with tinnitus describe the constant presence of noises like buzzing, roaring, hissing, and whistling. To some, it can even take the form of a high-pitched screech. This nerve-racking condition can significantly impair the ability to concentrate on the spoken message. The American Tinnitus Association (ATA) claims that over twelve million Americans suffer from this malady in its severe form, and others experience it to a lesser degree. There is no cure at this time, but some medications and tinnitus retraining can significantly improve the ability to cope with the disorder.

If you or others suspect you have a hearing problem, or if you experience tinnitus or a progressive hearing loss, see an ear doctor and an audiologist. They can best help you determine what treatment would be most beneficial. Until then, turn down the TV, close the door, or find a quiet place so you can *hear* what is being said. If you are hearing impaired, don't be shy about asking your conversation partner to speak clearly and a bit louder. Particularly on the telephone, distinct pronunciation is often more helpful to the hearing-impaired person than increasing the volume, which may only distort the message. If you have hearing-impaired family or friends, speaking clearly and facing your listener saves you from repeating and straining your voice. Best of all, this gesture creates a communication link that may be otherwise lost.

One of the most obstinate barriers to listening and one that virtually slams the door on the speaker is the issue of **status.** This reminds me of a story about job titles. One day the Governor of Kyoto paid a visit to Zen Master Keichu. The governor's visit was announced by an attendant who presented the master with a card that read, "Kitagaki, Governor of Kyoto." "I have no business with such a fellow," Keichu snapped. When the attendant relayed Keichu's response to the governor, the governor took a pen and scratched out the words *Governor of Kyoto* and handed the card back. When Keichu saw the card, he exclaimed, "Oh—Kitagaki! I'd love to see him!"

Status gets in the way of listening between rich and poor, doctors and patients, and managers and staff. I once knew a manager of a large department who, as part of his power trip, ordered his staff to follow him down the hall as they asked questions or presented ideas. He rarely made eye contact with his subordinates and walked past them as they spoke. Yet, when conversing with his peers or those higher on the administrative ladder, a dramatic change in his voice and body language took place. He looked them in the eye and smiled, nodding his head at any comment or suggestion. He laughed uproariously at their jokes and thanked them profusely for their unique insights (many of which his staff had voiced earlier and which he had ignored or dismissed). Unfortunately, this manager's transformation was most evident to his staff. His method of managing people was control and the assertion of *status* as a way to force cooperation. As a result, staff turnover was high and morale was low.

If we want to encourage loyalty, creative input, and positive attitudes from our employees, our kids, or our customers, we need to treat each individual with courtesy and respect. We do that by acknowledging that every person, by virtue of sheer life experience, has valuable insight to share. We all need to know that our opinions are valued.

Listening to what motivates employees helps them to excel in what they do best, thus creating a happier, more fulfilling work environment. By sitting down and facing our speakers, we value them. Not interrupting and keeping eye contact shows our respect. Reinforcing their contribution produces a feeling of idea sharing. Sam Walton, the late retail business tycoon and founder of Wal-Mart stores, said, "The key to success is to get out into the store and listen to what the associates have to say. It's terribly important for everyone to get involved. Our best ideas come from clerks and stock boys." By neutralizing the status discrepancy in this manner, we foster an atmosphere of communal vested interest and positive morale.

Many of us feel inferior to our doctors. Dr. Bernard Lown, in his wonderful book, *The Lost Art of Healing*, says, "To heal requires a relationship marked by equality." Can you imagine a situation more crucial to listening than talking with your physician about your health? Some of us feel belittled by a physician's status, and we often feel too intimidated to ask for an explanation or share concerns about our health. Other times, it is the fault of an individual doctor's poor bedside manner that makes us, as patients, feel insignificant. We may perceive that we're being looked down upon and may not feel comfortable sharing pertinent information that could lead to a diagnosis. In a litigation-prone system such as healthcare, health professionals in particular must practice good listening. Patients are less likely to sue when they feel that the doctor's treatment decision was motivated by concern for them. Any competitive healthcare organization is well aware of this need to be sensitive to the communication needs of its employees and patients.

At a recent gathering, I overheard the following remarks from a pleased customer: "Wow, that service manager at X Company was terrific! I wish I had started with them in the first place. She actually listened to me without interrupting! It took her ten minutes to fix the problem and I was on my way!" X Company has learned that listening shows respect and, even more than a free cup of coffee or a clean bathroom, respect for the customer leads to repeat business. The feeling of being appreciated as a customer stands out in stark contrast to the impersonal, give-me-a-break service attitude that dominates the marketplace today. In business, the more distance we put between us and our customers, the more they will stray towards the feel-good businesses and services. They may choose our business because we're faster, but resent the way we treat them. All it takes is for somebody to come around the corner who is faster—and friendly— and you're toast.

Some of us are uncomfortable with the idea of putting aside our egos to really listen and experience another's perspective. It may make us vulnerable to step out of the role we have learned to play. We may feel it is too risky to get close to our subordinates, clients, or family members. Or perhaps we fear losing our objectivity. It is the self-actualized individual, however, according to psychologist Abraham Maslow, who is secure enough with herself to demonstrate her wide potential as a communicator. The person on her way to becoming self-actualized is comfortable enough to mind-meld with others without fear of losing her sense of self. This ability springs, not from applying techniques learned in some seminar, but from a stable self-image and genuine respect for another's perspective. (I will discuss more about self-actualization later.)

Listening to ourselves, choosing words and tone of voice that facilitate an understanding with our conversation partner, can help break down the status barrier. For example, do you frequently use professional jargon or vocabulary with clients who are not in your line of work? Might anyone perceive your tone as condescending or cold? Intentionally "swinging the lingo" is the ultimate tool of information control that alienates the consultant from the customer. Using unfamiliar words on purpose is the opposite of communicating. It can be a major barrier to a satisfying customer interaction. Unfortunately, the receivers of shop talk, when they are not from the same shop, frequently nod their heads, not wanting to appear ignorant, and leave the office with a sense of helplessness. The insensitive consultant, on the other hand, may be totally convinced that he has not only impressed the customer, but that the customer actually understood what he had to say.

As a rule of thumb, if you are spoken to in this manner, say to the consultant, "Excuse me, but I am not a lawyer (accountant, doctor). Please use laymen's terms so I can understand what you are talking about." Whenever I do this, I usually get a translation that makes me more knowledgeable and satisfied with the service. It also saves time. (Coincidentally, it can be a wake-up call to the consultant. He gets the message that you're there to get your money's worth, not to be impressed. He may choose his words more carefully with the next client.)

Public speakers looking to promote their services or educate the public need to avoid this communication pitfall. Prior to the engagement find out about your audience. How well do they know your topic? Chances are, they would not be coming to listen to you speak if they already knew your buzz words as well as you. Be sure to at least define the jargon in simple terms before you get too deep into your lecture.

If any of these status barriers get in the way of your understanding the message and getting the message across to others, begin by applying the golden rule of listening: listen to others as you would have others to listen to you. And, if you are a consultant, please speak to others as you would like to be spoken to.

As soon as we meet someone for the first time, we start to evaluate whether or not they are worth listening to. If she doesn't meet certain personal criteria, her words become fainter and fainter until only our thoughts fill our attention. Some people's checklists include **race, gender, and age prejudice.** Some of us judge according to dress or **physical appearance.** Many a fund-raiser can attest to the fact that, at times, the least best dressed is often the inconspicuous donor for the new children's cancer center. Preferential listening based on such shallow biases can cost millions in mistaken identities and sex-discrimination law suits.

One of the most common obstacles to listening comes in the form of physical handicaps. As children we may have been taught to feel sorry for those who were lame, disfigured, or blind. It was impolite to stare at such people, a courtesy we resisted because of fear or curiosity. Interaction with a handicapped person with communication deficits may have caused us to assume that a disabled body means a disabled mind. Such stereotypes can persist into adulthood. Those of us in the healthcare field are fortunate to have broken through this barrier to some extent, although many disabled people would agree that their physical condition often discourages even healthcare professionals from taking other medical concerns seriously. As handicapped access becomes more common in public places, our opportunities for interaction with disabled persons are on the rise. More people with disabilities are overcoming these stereotypes by speaking out in the media. Christopher Reeves, the actor who sustained a spinal cord injury following a fall from a horse, and Stephen Hawking, physicist and author of *A Brief History of Time*, wheelchair bound by Lou

Gehrig's disease, and Michael J. Fox, the actor with Parkinson's disease, have not allowed their disabilities to be sheltered from the public eye. They have helped to dispel faulty notions about the physically handicapped population. My experience is that there are more able-bodied people with communication handicaps than there are people with physical handicaps. The true handicap lies in our perception of the individual. This applies to all the barriers to better listening.

Other times we allow negative **past experiences** with a person to interfere, or we might experience a feeling of immediate dislike for no apparent reason. (Maybe, we tell ourselves, she was our worst enemy in a past life!) Try not to let past experience contaminate the present. Use past experience to help you learn about the world and how to avoid repeating your mistakes. Do not, however, rely blindly on previous experience to evaluate a present situation. This builds barriers between us and our speakers. We assume, for example, that we know what this person is going to say, so we really don't have to listen. Parents and spouses frequently complain of this phenomenon. We tune out familiar messages, particularly those associated with criticism and household chores, and attend only the novel and desirable messages. Expanding our response styles (chapter five) will help to decrease the selective listening in our household and at the workplace.

Some of the most crucial information to be gained as listeners—like people's names—gets lost while we are in the midst of acceptability checklists. It is essential for us to become aware of the extent to which these obstacles interfere. Our challenge is to drive that discriminating force toward a positive end. See these differences between people as invitations to broaden our spectrum of possible points of view. Every time we truly listen to people different from ourselves, they give us an opportunity to see a view through another window. This mindset expands our creative potential. An overly judgmental and critical approach diminishes our scope of possibilities.

Let me say a few words about being judgmental. Of course we are judgmental when we listen to others. We may be able to put our biases aside, but we still evaluate to some extent, especially when decisions have to be made. In fact, our survival depends on such critical evaluation. If we were not selective to some extent, we wouldn't think twice about picking up a stranger on the highway, ingesting certain substances, or engaging in risky or unethical activities. Learning from past experience also saves us from wasting time. Our ability to get to work and back in one piece, hold onto our jobs, and be responsible parents depends on our ability to judge situations and act accordingly. But at what point does survival judgment stop and our biases and closed-mindedness begin? When does the healthy instinct to discriminate become self-limiting and unfair to others?

In studying the descriptions of my students' thought processes when listening, it appears that judgment evolves through different stages. The first stage is general recognition of the person talking (Do I know—or know of—this person?). This observation may be related to the first-fifteen-seconds phenomenon reported by image consultants. According to these experts, we make hard and fast decisions about people during the first fifteen seconds of contact. These first fifteen seconds may be part of our normal, healthy survival judgment. With some, however, this brief period of evaluation is reflexive. Thus, we may have great difficulty in eliminating this knee-jerk response.

When we are deciding whether to listen, however, our barriers kick in fairly early. Immediately, a person's physical appearance triggers a whole list of possible judgment calls, good and bad. The speaker's voice and mannerisms may set off another chain of prejudices. If we cling to any one of these biases in depth, we run the risk of missing the content of the person's message.

My theory is that the extraordinary listener does not allow her attention to be consumed by any bias. She acknowledges the presence of certain learned barriers, but turns her attention to what that person has to say and the feelings behind the message. A student said it best, "Putting aside your biases and tuning into the speaker are like tuning in a radio station to receive a clear signal with no distortion."

Judgments and criticisms, if allowed to overtake the interaction, are destructive to the relationship and the potential opportunities that exist between speaker and listener. Judgment creeps into our psyches at an early age. We show preferences for certain toys, learn to be picky about food, select TV over homework. As adults, certain activities are earmarked as enjoyable or distasteful with varying degrees of acceptance in between. Procrastination, another self-limiting behavior, is in large part due to the relentless discrimination between what we need to get done and what we want to do at the moment. The habits of harsh judgment and negative discrimination are at the heart of our inability to genuinely listen to people. How can we begin to break down these barriers?

Les Kaye, the author of *Zen at Work,* a teacher of Zen, and a former IBM executive, writes about seeing each activity of the day as equally necessary and important. This is the Zen concept of equanimity or even-mindedness. To cling to the mindset that there are distinctly desirable and undesirable activities and people creates distress and anxiety. We go through life trying to decide in which mental box a particular person or activity belongs—good or bad, right or wrong, interesting or boring. This attitude puts limits on our flexibility of thought and openness to new ideas.

Alan Watts said, "Good without evil is like up without down, and . . . to make an ideal of pursuing the good is like trying to get rid of the left by turning constantly to the right. One is therefore compelled to go round in circles." In a footnote, Watts mentioned that there was a politician in San Francisco who so detested the political left that he would go to great inconvenience when driving to avoid making a left turn.

Accepting the notion that our daily activities are interrelated, no matter how trivial, is one way to dissolve some of the barriers to listening. Kaye says that concern for efficiency in each activity (versus concern for achieving goals) facilitates the flowing nature of work. In this approach, he says, "Work became like a garden, with new and interesting shapes, textures, and fragrances at each turn. Problems and difficulties did not go away, but my relationship with work was different."

One recent autumn, my father and I took a weekday vacation and went mountain biking in Franconia Notch, New Hampshire. The weather was beautiful, and along our path were waterfalls, natural rock formations, and a forest full of color. The air was clear and fresh. I returned from that day trip suffused with a sense of peaceful satisfaction. As I reflected recently on this experience, I realized how I have changed as a result of dissolving some of my barriers. The sense of satisfaction I experience when making a connection with a patient or coworker is similar to the sense of connection with nature that I experienced biking through that mountain paradise.

In the past, I might have seen this day trip as getting away from the rat race and leaving it all behind. Now my sense is that work and nonwork activities are both deserving of time and attention. To realize the equality of satisfaction between two formerly disparate activities was a taste of enlightenment. Instead of critiquing and comparing, I now see the slender thread of connection between all activities. It has made me less judgmental and critical, and has made me a more balanced and positive person.

If we can dissolve our hard and fast judgments of people based on their attitudes, styles, and points of view, we can then begin to see each person as equally essential to the workings of life: the guy who dumps your garbage is as integral to the process of living as the brain surgeon who eliminates your dizziness.

A few years back I had a patient with an extreme case of people discrimination. John was a middle-aged administrative assistant for a computer firm. He was referred to me by a psychologist. He had a history of depression associated with attention deficit disorder since childhood. John was extremely knowledgeable and intelligent despite test results that showed marked difficulties with listening and memory. He had benefited significantly from a combination of counseling and medication, but still had major difficulties with his coworkers.

Aside from being a poor listener, he showed little ability to hear himself. He spoke endlessly and appeared totally unaware when others tried to join in. He did not perceive his interminable monologues as rude and showed no interest in letting anyone else speak. In addition, he often drifted from the subject and rarely answered a question directly. I could see why John was never invited to participate on a team or given advancement opportunities at work, or why, despite his vast technical knowledge, his job was at stake.

After some discussion and a few roleplaying activities directed towards heightening his awareness, John admitted that he was torn between having to get along with people to make a salary and his unyielding perception that *no one else at his workplace was worth listening to.* No one there knew as much as he knew, and it was a "waste of time" to hear from the others. It was clear that for John to improve his listening skills, he would have to curb his ego and learn to value the opinions of his coworkers.

John is a dramatic example of how even the most sophisticated skills and strategies are doomed to failure unless we can develop the attitude of openness essential to mindful listening. Choosing to see our conversation partners as equals is the mindset needed to be an effective listener.

Another major impediment to listening is the emphasis we place on getting to **our personal agendas.** Let's say you have just been introduced to the new CEO of the company. As she tells you about herself and her intentions for the company, you may find yourself formulating your mission statement and chomping at the bit to introduce yourself and your interests. You want her to like you, so you wear your best smile, straighten your collar, nod frequently, and try to act in a professional manner. Finally, when it is your time to speak, your content bears little or no relationship to the new CEO's agenda. Because the only thing you paid attention to was your own agenda, you leave the meeting having learned nothing.

This approach to accomplishing goals leads only to frustration and low self-esteem. The more productive method of communicating our interests would be to sit back and make an effort to listen. Learn about this person and be alert to commonalties or differences between her plans and your concerns. Notice her manner, pace, and style. What are her priorities? Are yours in there somewhere? Make her agenda your agenda. When it is your turn to speak, indicate that you have carefully considered her message by making a connection between her interests and yours. Stick to the need-to-know facts and keep it short. Let her ask for more information. When she learns that you are a thoughtful listener, chances are that she will be open to you in the future. A reputation for emphasizing your own agenda above the interests of the group makes you an unlikely pick for team projects or positions that require flexibility, vision, and leadership.

When meeting a new customer, you may feel pressed to take control of the meeting and start out by telling the customer what you can do for him. You are **focused on the outcome** of the meeting—usually the sale—instead of the process of cultivating a relationship. Instead, if you recall from your Business 101 course, let the customer tell you his needs and concerns; let him focus on his agenda first. Then you will be better able to use your agenda to make a happy customer. Why is it important to put aside your agenda when listening to someone else? So that you can hear what the other party is saying. This requires mental flexibility. If you focus only on your own needs, you'll miss opportunities for a successful outcome.

Harvey Mackay, the legendary salesman, best-selling author, and motivational speaker, believes that the strong personal relationships that he developed over the years transformed an ailing manufacturing company into a revenue-generating workhorse. At a speakers' seminar a few years back in Boston, I recall standing in line to get some advice from Mr. Mackay. Before I could ask my question, he got me to talk about myself. He had such an intense way of listening that I found myself divulging personal information quite voluntarily. He made note of this information and succinctly answered my question, which was well worth the twenty minutes I spent standing in line. He not only answered my question, he linked the answer to how I could use the information in a creative way given *my* circumstances. In a matter of a few minutes I felt indebted to him because of the effort he made to get to know me and solve my problem in a personal way. Wouldn't we like all our clients to feel that way about us?

In *Success* magazine (February 1999), Mackay reveals how he acquired the skill to establish relationships through listening. He says, "My father handed me a Rolodex when I was eighteen and said, 'Every person you meet for the rest of your life goes into this. You add a little something about them on the back of the card—family, hobbies, et cetera. And you cultivate that Rolodex like a garden.'" Mackay says this information is essential to sales work, because "people buy from people, and the more you know about them, the more they're flattered, the more they're at ease—and the more they buy."

This advice was clearly unknown to the customer relations manager at my car dealership from whom I received a form letter. Keep in mind that I only service my car there, I have never *purchased* a car from them. It opened by thanking me for servicing my car there a few weeks earlier, which was fine. It went on in the second paragraph to tell how only 100 percent customer satisfaction with their technical service is acceptable. That was standard fare also. But the closing paragraph said, "Our relationships really do begin *after* the sale is made. We value *those* relationships and look forward to your allowing us to continue to serve you." If that's what they really believe, I can bet that when I walk in there to have my car serviced or to shop for a new car, I'll be treated like a number or worse, like a steak—until, of course, *after* the sale.

Listening to establish a relationship with anyone, whether customer, friend, or family member, requires that our concentration be flexible enough to shift into receiver mode and stay there, instead of being distracted by our agendas. (We will discuss in chapter five a way to do that.)

Stephen Covey, in a commentary in his book, *The Seven Habits of Highly Effective People,* calls listening "the magical habit." He suggests our goal should be to "listen first to understand." A good listener sees himself as the receiver rather than the taker. He must not impose himself on the speaker, but instead let the speaker's words flow in on him. Otherwise, the listener's prejudices and expectations will interfere and cloud the message and intent of the messenger. This is the difference between self-serving, egocentric listening and patient, selfless listening. It doesn't take a smart person to sense the difference between someone who listens in order to gain something and one who listens to build a relationship.

If you are a goal-oriented individual, then consider a loftier goal than just making the sale. Strive to build a strong working relationship with customers or coworkers by listening. The sale may not be immediate, but if and when it does occur, it will yield greater satisfaction for all parties and greater potential for profits. You become more flexible in your thinking because you are less discriminating, and therefore open to the opportunities and ideas that may present themselves.

Efforts to put aside our self-interest to really listen to someone else are often thwarted by other thoughts. At any given moment our attention is focused on thoughts external to the self, such as "It's raining again today," or "Interest rates are dropping." Internal thoughts may sound like "I'm thirsty," "I'm really out of shape," or "I hope the boss likes this report." A steady stream of internal focusing blocks our ability to listen. It is very easy to nod our heads and *act* like we are listening when actually we are consumed by our internal jabber.

A constructive dose of self-awareness is a good thing. Thinking about ourselves, analyzing our actions, and planning our behavior have helped us achieve personal success. This book encourages close self-study in order to make changes that enhance personal growth. But this positive initiative can become a negative force if our attention shifts from developing our potential to the discrepancy between standards set by others (how we should look, act, and achieve) and what we see in the mirror.

Numerous reports suggest that self-awareness can be a negative experience. Internal brooding interferes with creativity, the ability to relax, and openness to experience. In 1982, a study by Mihaly Csikszentmihalyi of the University of Chicago, *Self-Awareness and Aversive Experience,* sought to explore the effect of self-awareness in natural settings. One hundred and seven employees from five large companies, ranging from assembly line workers to managers and engineers, volunteered to participate in the study. Volunteers were given electronic pagers to carry all day. The pagers emitted signals randomly seven to nine times a day during regular waking hours. When subjects were beeped, they were required to fill out a short questionnaire regarding their activity, thoughts, and moods at the moment. Responses were ranked according to whether these thoughts dealt with self-concerns or external concerns like food and work. Subjects were also asked about the quality of the experience at the given moment: feeling 1) happy and cheerful, 2) alert and active, or 3) involved. The results showed that internal thinking is a particularly unpleasant experience, since focusing on the self was ranked lowest across all three aspects of quality. Thoughts about other people and conversation were reported to be significantly more pleasant and active. It is fair to conclude that instead of dwelling on self-assessment (usually filled with negative self-talk), we might be happier listening to someone else.

How many times a day do you find yourself thinking, "I don't believe I said that!", "How stupid!", "What an idiot!", "I look terrible today," or "I know I will not be able to remember all that he's telling me." Sound familiar? By proclaiming our deficiencies in **negative self-talk,** even silently to ourselves, we chip away at our self-confidence. Negative self-talk attacks our feelings of self-worth. By increasing our anxiety, these internal distractions prevent us from focusing our attention on the message and the messenger.

Anxiety breeds fatigue and depression, both of which deter effective listening. Negative self-talk saps our energy and weakens our enthusiasm for initiating and completing tasks, whether they be cold-calling, solving a problem, or arranging for that interview. Perpetuation of self-directed put-downs limits the range of opportunities we allow ourselves to experience.

Chances are, if we tally our ratio of negative comments to positive comments, it will be strikingly skewed to the negative side. One way to rid yourself of this self-defeating behavior is to balance out a negative comment with a positive one. Every time you say something like, "Gee, that was a dumb thing I said," counter it *immediately* with something positive like, "Next time I'll choose my words more carefully. Perhaps I could have said it another way," or "My presentation on Thursday really went well; I was very concise."

In our efforts to improve our listening, it is important that we examine our behavior as objectively as possible. Only then can we make changes that are welcome to ourselves and those around us. Negative self-talk starts to take over when we lose objectivity about our weak points. We dwell on the weak points and neglect the positive ones. A negative self-image sprouts from attaching too much importance to occasional lapses like forgetting our keys or making a careless error on a test. Instead of calling yourself stupid or an idiot, take a deep breath, accept the mistake as part of the human experience, and resolve to learn from it. Then feel the disgust and irritation fade.

The more lengthy and severe a beating we give ourselves, the less time we have for listening to constructive and rational input. That negative inner voice is not a helpful guide, but a self-destructive force that can lead to tragic ends. It is useful to ask who that negative voice sounds like. Could it be the voice of a verbally abusive parent or an overly condemning spouse we could never please? Negative self-talk can be so pervasive that it distracts us from processing the spoken message. Instead of taking in words and meaning, we think, "I wonder if I have bad breath?" or "What will I say if he asks me about that project I haven't started yet?" Others perceive our lack of confidence through our posture, eye contact, and vocal characteristics. Negative self-talk sets us up for negative treatment by others. Remember the words of the famous First Lady Eleanor Roosevelt: "No one on the face of this earth can make you feel inferior without your permission."

Getting to know our personal barriers and the energy we waste trying to reinforce them is the next step in becoming better listeners. When I encounter a barrier, I discuss it aloud with myself. I also voice any supporting arguments that contribute to this way of thinking. Often, hearing my weak argument for upholding a barrier is enough to dispel it. Sometimes my reasons make me laugh. Other times, I'm disappointed with how selfish I sound. In every instance, however, I at least try to acknowledge my resistance, and over time, resolve to work through it whenever it comes up.

Sometimes we have to be satisfied with a slow chiseling away of obstacles to better communication. After all, it took a lifetime to create them. Cleaning house of these unhelpful judgments, however, makes room for new learning and personal growth. It is also one of the best ways to get to know ourselves.

Becoming aware of our barriers to the message or the messenger helps us to better understand, and in some cases, accept the barriers of others toward us. Many of the barriers discussed in this chapter reflect the diversity present in our culture. Beliefs, customs, and behaviors vary not only between persons from different countries but between persons from the same country. If you have ever worked at a job where employees in one department were very easygoing and team oriented, but in another department were more rigid and less interactive, you have experienced minicultures within a larger culture. To further complicate the variety, there can be people of twenty or more different nationalities working together in one corporation. They also have their unique biases towards gender, seniority, race, and work ethic.

Identifying our barriers is easy. Conquering them is another matter. Trying to eliminate our barriers one by one is a painstakingly difficult process. We cannot expect ourselves to reprogram reflexive ways of thinking that have been ingrained since childhood. Applying mindful listening every day, however, can diminish their potency and open our minds.

A global approach to softening our barriers is to think of listening as a way of building a sense of community. According to Zen tradition, we are all connected as living beings; we are cousins with every living thing in the universe. This concept is called *sangha.* If we listen with *sangha,* in the belief that we are all connected, it is easier to be respectful and patient. When we honor our speakers in this way, we also show respect and tolerance for ourselves. Conversely, when we shut out others due to our biases, we also hurt ourselves.

Networking is a modern application of *sangha.* We make contacts with others in our professional communities and, because we share similar interests, listen to them in a special way. Networking sessions or support groups are usually positive exchanges, not a setting for putting down one another. Town meetings, fund-raising activities, and religious services take place in the spirit of connecting with one another toward some positive end. It is heartening to see an increase of interfaith and cross-cultural celebrations designed to enhance understanding and respect for the beliefs and heritages of others in our local communities. Participation in such events can expedite the mental housecleaning necessary in order to become mindful listeners. This global mindset will calm an overly critical ear, particularly in situations when it is necessary for us to listen.

Crack a Few Walls

1. Noise is ever present in our environment. Hone your auditory discrimination skills by purposely turning down the volume on the TV just when you want to turn it up. Leave the sound of the dishwasher and the dog barking in the background and put all your attention on what the person on TV is saying. This also challenges your ability to concentrate in noisy situations that are not under your control.

2. Two or three times a week, open your mind to something you've previously opposed and don't know much about. For example, I used to dislike football, based on preconceived notions about the type of people who play football and those who watch it. But I had never taken the time to really watch a game and look for the good in it. So one day I said to myself, "If football is so popular,

maybe I'm not giving it a chance." I turned on a Buffalo Bills game for about thirty minutes, and I discovered at least three things that make football interesting and entertaining. Even though it may never be my favorite sport, I now understand the attraction to football and I am less critical about the sport. Try this approach with your not-so-favorite things or people. Be open to their views and listen to them from the standpoint that there is, at least, something to learn from them. As you widen your knowledge base, you will grow to appreciate these various perspectives as valid as your own.

3. Here's one of my favorite listening activities. Try this at a company outing or some large gathering. When you get into a conversation with someone, keep the conversation away from *your* agenda. Ask a few open-ended questions that begin with *why, what,* or *how* to get the other person talking, for example, "How did you get interested in fly-fishing?" or "What do you think is a wise investment?" Your aim is not to see how many questions you can ask, but to let others do more of the talking and you, more of the listening. At the end of the day, notice how much you learned and how many new acquaintances you made simply by giving others the spotlight.

4. Identify people in your life whom you dislike. Facing your prejudices or strong dislikes, whatever they may be and for whatever reason they exist, is an unpleasant task for most of us. Now, find one thing you like or respect about that person or activity. The next time you

interact with him, focus on that one thing. Most likely, your negative judgment will also compete for your attention. Acknowledge its presence and refocus your thoughts back to the positive aspect.

5. Over the next few days, notice how often negative thoughts about yourself or others creep into your mind. The longer you dwell on negative thoughts, the more deeply they become ingrained. Counteract these negative thoughts with positive ones.

6. To broaden your perspective on any given topic, try this eye-opening activity. Pick up a popular magazine with a wide readership, like *Time* or *Newsweek*. Read the featured article, which is usually several pages. Think about your opinion of the article: the writer's point of view, the tone, the accuracy or credibility of named sources. Were the points well supported? Get the next issue of the same magazine and read the letters from readers. Even if the article was not particularly controversial you will read at least four points of view different from yours. If you have time, go back and reread the article, keeping other readers' comments in mind. It may be startling to see something you missed or interpreted differently. Whether you agree or disagree is not the point. What's important is to accept these observations as valid perceptions.

7. You cannot will yourself to stop judging and criticizing others, but you can stop and analyze it when it occurs. Examine the foundation for not wanting to listen to

a particular person or idea. Which barriers are operating? Perhaps you adopted these responses from a TV personality, a parent, or a mentor. If you trace it back to the source you may find it has no reasonable basis. You may start laughing when you try to reason it out loud, "Well, my mother would never have permitted me to talk about those things," or "It's not respectful to question my doctor's opinion or ask for an explanation." The origins of our barriers are usually flimsy and out of context. Other times, the basis for our reactions has more substance, but is still from another time and place. For example, if an old boss with whom you had some difficult times in the past visits your office to discuss a new project, notice how instantaneously those memories come back to haunt you. You may find yourself prejudging what she is going to say and criticizing the timing of her visit. Tell yourself, "I see how I am thinking of those past experiences with Amy right now. I will put them aside and listen openly to what she has to say. This time may be different." In this way you take control of your barriers instead of letting them interfere with a potential opportunity for growth or reconciliation.

8. At least once a day when you're listening to a co-worker relate a story, set aside your evaluative self. Be a witness to his ideas. Notice how your barriers want to kick in and start judging. When this happens, put your mind in neutral and simply observe.

9. As a way of re-examining some of the snap decisions and judgments we make during the day, Zen Master

Thich Nhat Hanh suggests copying the question, "Are you sure?" on a piece of paper and taping it to a wall. Great opportunities are often lost to the snap-decision maker who failed to open his mind to find the golden nugget of potential in an idea.

Mindful Listening

Zen Master Seung Sahn said it best in a poem: "If in this lifetime/ You do not open your mind/You cannot digest/Even one drop of water."

The best way I know to open the mind and clean house of the noise and barriers that sabotage our capacity to listen is meditation. Zen means "meditation practice." There are several different ways to meditate, but here I will describe Zen meditation, also known as *zazen*. I also refer to meditation as *breathing practice*.

Meditation does not cause us to be dull, listless, or emotionally detached. On the contrary, it unleashes positive physical and mental energy held captive by stress and anxiety. It brings us to a level of relaxed awareness, which is the first step in harnessing the destructive tendencies of the barriers to listening.

After even a few weeks of meditation practice, you will find that your tendency to overreact in the face of your barriers is less. If your spouse starts complaining about money, you'll be less apt to shout back or use hurtful words. Instead of creating more negative energy you'll be able to rechannel that energy in a more positive way— talking through solutions, feelings, and other needs that may be at the root of the complaint. If you make a mistake or a bad decision, you can simply acknowledge it, learn what you can about it, resolve to avoid repeating it, and put it aside. This more constructive use of energy stimulates personal growth. Dwelling ad nauseum on mistakes and past experiences drains your energy and perpetuates low self-esteem.

Every person is born with a mental space, in inner area of the mind reserved for peaceful contemplation. However, over time this space becomes like a closet where we've thrown outworn clothes, warped records, and broken tools. We may want to hang something new and beautiful there, but there's simply no more room.

The Zen masters promote meditation as a way of emptying the mind of clutter and unproductive thoughts to make space for personal growth. As it pertains to listening, meditation allows our minds to hear with less distortion new ideas and points of view. After a few weeks of practice you will notice that you are less anxious when hearing ideas that differ from your point of view. Your ability to concentrate is deeper and more enduring, and with anxiety under control, you can better focus your attention on getting and retaining the message. Moreover, regular meditation practice improves your attitude, the ability to deploy attention, and sets the stage for mindful listening.

Meditation costs no money and is free of religious bias. It is simply the most natural way to connect your new way of thinking with the way you listen. Calmness, an open mind, and focused attention are the foundation for mindful listening. Here and in subsequent chapters I will describe a few different ways to meditate. For some of you, this first step, as simple as it seems, will be the greatest challenge to your commitment to become a better listener.

Here is a basic method I use for daily practice. I prefer to meditate for thirty to forty minutes at a time, twice a day. When you are just starting out, ten minutes is fine. It is best to practice daily, even for short periods. As you start to experience the benefits of meditation, you may want to extend your meditation time. To avoid falling asleep during practice, do not meditate right after eating. Therefore, early in the morning and before dinnertime are ideal.

Choose a quiet spot free of distractions. Sit in a solid but comfortable chair or get a cushion for sitting cross-legged on the floor. A firm cushion called a *zafu* is traditionally used during Zen meditation. As a meditation teacher once told me, "Sit up straight, dignified like a tree, but with shoulders and arms soft at your side." Rest your hands on your thighs with palms up or down. There are several hand positions. When I began meditating, I preferred to sit in a half-lotus position with my hands on my knees, palms up. I liked to think that this position inspired me to be more open-minded and receptive to different perspectives.

Begin your meditation by keeping your eyes slightly open and gaze down at a forty-five-degree angle. You may keep your eyes closed, but you risk daydreaming and falling asleep. Breathe in and out through your nose, deeply and slowly. Feel your breath move in and out of your body. To check your pace, count slowly up to three seconds as you inhale and exhale for three seconds or more. Do not hold your breath. Keep your mind's eye and ear on the breath. Other thoughts will sneak into your mind. You may start thinking about your grocery list, an upcoming meeting, or a hundred other concerns. As soon as you notice these intrusions, acknowledge their presence, let them pass, and get back to watching your breath. Do not become impatient with yourself for straying from the focus on the breath, this happens to everyone. Simply guide your focus back to the breath. If you find it difficult to stay focused at first, try counting your breaths silently. Inhale on one, exhale on one; inhale on two, exhale on two, and so on. When you get to ten, start over again at one. If you find yourself sneaking peeks at your clock to check the time, set a timer with a gentle alarm or ask someone to softly knock on the door to let you know it is time to stop. When you are finished with your practice, gradually open your eyes completely and stay seated for a minute or two. Slowly stand up and continue with your regular activities.

Another popular way to stay with the breath utilizes visual imagery. As you inhale slowly through your nose, picture inhaling positive energy from a glowing star overhead. As you fill your lungs with air, see this star filling your mind with goodwill and happy feelings. As you exhale slowly, think of cleansing your mind and your body of the wasted energy that supports petty jealousies, irrational biases toward others, and negative self-talk. Allow only goodwill and self-confidence to remain.

Start to open your mind to your *sangha*, the community of people you come in contact with every day. This helps to neutralize your barriers or bad feelings toward those to whom you have the greatest difficulty listening. Toward the end of your meditation, as your breathing becomes shallow, think of wishing your friends and family well. For the moment, let go of any negative feelings between you and them. Go on to wish your coworkers and customers well. Finally, think of the people you are uneasy with and wish them well too, in the spirit that we are all members of a very large family put here to help each other.

Breathing practice or meditation can be more contemplative at times, particularly when we are in conflict of some sort. These are the moments when we can begin to dissolve barriers. I liken this process to a solid block of sandstone sitting in a pool of water. Slowly over time, that block begins to break apart in chunks and ultimately, particle by particle. Contemplative meditation allows us to detoxify some of our most powerful negative emotions.

For example, if you have been working diligently on a project for a long time without success and a friend, Max, experiences overnight success with something that took him only a few days to put together, you may feel disappointment at first. The status barrier may make it very hard to listen to him talk about his success. Then the negative self-talk barrier kicks in, and from these two come resentment and jealousy. During a contemplative meditation, you might go back to the feelings of disappointment you felt when you heard the news: *What is at the root of my disappointment? Jealousy over money? His better house? His fame? Are these the reasons I started my project? Are these things necessities for me and my family? Would I really be happier with those things? Why would I deny Max his success and happiness? If the tables were turned, how would I want him to feel? Defeated? Cheated? Would that make me feel prouder of my accomplishment? Is there any good that can come from Max's success? How can I learn from his experience? If I never achieve success, will anything bad happen to me? Can I listen to Max and other successful people any easier now?*

In this way, meditation can transform your barriers into open doors to self-transformation, creativity, and wisdom. Negative emotions stemming from these barriers only impede personal growth. Breaking down barriers can be an uncomfortable process, but a process you must go through to become a better listener. As a Zen monk and coauthor of *The Monk and the Philosopher*, Matthieu Ricard, said, "Actions are born from thoughts. Without mastering your thoughts, you cannot master your actions."

Make a habit of several minutes of quiet meditation every day. To listen well, you have to first settle down the internal noise. Think of your mind as a glassful of water and sand. Shake up this container and notice how the mix of sand and water makes it difficult to see through. Let the container sit for several minutes and watch how, as the sand settles to the bottom, the water clears. This is essentially what happens in our bodies during breathing practice. After a few sessions, you will emerge from your meditation feeling more mentally balanced. This settled feeling state, free of internal clutter, is the ideal state for new learning. You will start to notice this sense of relaxation extending to several minutes and eventually to hours. Your threshold for becoming annoyed will increase. As you become more consistent in meditation practice, this state of balance can be maintained for longer periods, enabling you to focus and listen better.

Contrary to meditation myths, this practice will not make you apathetic or indifferent, nor will it alienate you from your environment and the people around you. It will, however, help you to become detached from the excess emotional upheaval and interference generated by your barriers.

Chapter Five

What's Their Movie?

To study the way of the Buddha is to study your own self.
To study your own self is to forget yourself.
To forget yourself is to have the objective world prevail in you.
—Master Dogen (1200-1253)

There are many reasons we find movies entertaining. We get a chance to escape our mundane, predictable lives and get into someone else's shoes. Good movies have a way of drawing us into the characters' consciousness, values, and lifestyle. We, the audience, empathize with the characters, often to the point of feeling their fear or sadness. We leave the theater with the thought that our connection with the characters, at least in a small way, has changed our lives. Our mood and our scope of understanding have been altered by forgetting ourselves for a while to view another's perspective. In real life, speakers often invite us to get into their movies with comments like, "Do you see it my way?" or "Put yourself in my place." If we approach a listening opportunity with the same self-abandonment as we do at the movies, think of how much more we stand to gain from those encounters.

The movie mindset is opposite to the act-like-you-are-listening approach, in which you mimic a listening posture, nod often, say "Mm-hmm," and maintain eye contact. How can you possibly make all these adjustments and still concentrate on the speaker? It is not that these actions are contrary to what you do when you really listen. But to focus on this list of body language to-dos risks appearing artificial to the speaker. Just like at the movies, when you forget yourself and get into the shoes of the speaker, your body *naturally* relaxes into listening posture. When you truly listen, you don't need to think about your posture or what you should be doing with your hands. Your gestures and expressions effortlessly reflect your interest. All you have to do is enjoy the adventure!

You take time to listen for many of the same reasons that you go to the movies—to satisfy your curiosity, to be informed, to be entertained, to get another point of view, to experience something outside yourself. Therefore, when you listen to another person, how simple it is to do nothing more than get into his movie!

My effectiveness as a clinician has improved much since I made it a habit to get into my patients' movies before delving into the test or treatment of the day. The movie mindset gives me a third ear to fully grasp the patient's reasons for coming to see me. A few minutes of listening to the patient or a family member tell me about himself, the patient's interests, and lifestyle give me that extra insight into their world that may make all the difference in our success as a team. They may volunteer their feelings about their physical handicaps or describe some of the other challenges they face. These comments are very helpful and save time in the treatment planning process. After getting into their movies and understanding how they see the world, I know better how to structure my therapy sessions. For example, if my patient has a history of being extremely organized and precise, I will present the information and his performance results in an outline format or graph. This way I remain flexible in my craft, the patient appreciates my sensitivity to his way of seeing the world, is more motivated to practice and comply with the recommendations, and will show faster improvement. Similar results can be achieved if I know my patient is an avid golfer. I will select articles on golfing and use golf lingo to make analogies between golf and the patient's performance on various therapy tasks. Getting into their movie not only makes people feel comfortable disclosing information that can affect the outcome, but also adds sparkle to what could otherwise be an ordinarily dull and less effective interaction. For this reason, the movie mindset is a win-win listening approach.

The movie mindset may be most needed with the people we have the hardest time relating to—our children. For example, your teenage daughter comes home after school, mumbles a few choice phrases about the basketball coach, rushes upstairs and slams the door to her room. You have two alternatives: 1) You could make matters worse by scolding her—after all, that particular show of disgust is not appropriate for a young lady; or 2) you could offer to share her movie and listen to her tell about her day. If you choose the latter action, you'll forget about the swearing and door slamming for awhile and put yourself in her place while she relives the day's miserable events. Just like at the movies, you put yourself aside and lock into the drama. What your teenager really needs is for you to relate to her perspective, her stage of maturity, her needs. If you stay tuned to her predicament and remain silent but attentive, she may reveal that her outburst was the result of the upcoming SAT test or not being asked to the homecoming dance.

Getting into the movie gives you the chance to identify with her frustration and disappointment. You empathize with your daughter. You look back at your own high-school days and recall a similar frustration after being chastised for arriving late at swim practice because of a big science project or an argument with your boyfriend. Your teenager senses your attempt to identify with her and breathes a sigh of relief. By withholding your usual parenting approach of scolding and advice, which would have alienated your daughter, you chose to strengthen your relationship by just being a good friend. (I will talk more in chapter seven about specific response styles that cut these valuable movies short.)

As mentioned in chapter two, your barriers are most resistant to change when you are self-absorbed. Getting into the movie of the speaker as she relates her troubles, predicaments, or triumphs is an easy and familiar way to give your barriers a back seat. But for some of us, the preoccupation with personal agenda and status gets in the way of connecting with others.

At work, it may be difficult to shed your armor and feel that you are doing your job. You may even think that some degree of coolness is needed to get the client to cooperate with you. We have been conditioned by our teachers to act superior or distance ourselves from our clients in order to gain their respect. It is, of course, important to communicate that you are experienced and knowledgeable. After all, your skill is what got you this job. Customers, like yourself, overwhelmingly prefer to connect in a symmetrical manner where people speak to each other as human being to human being, not top dog to underdog.

A good way to connect with customers and establish their trust is to reveal some information about yourself. As awkward as this may feel (self-disclosure may be regarded as unprofessional), telling your clients a bit about yourself sets the stage for a cooperative effort. For example, if I have a singer who is coming to me for voice therapy, I feel comfortable letting him know that I was an aspiring opera singer in college, and I can understand how difficult it is to pass up an important audition when you have laryngitis. I don't need to go into details; I just make a statement that indicates I can fully understand his predicament.

I have interviewed many singers and athletes who resist sound medical advice because they don't believe medical people can relate to their passion for singing or sport. They are more likely to accept the advice of a coach or mentor who may have less medical background but more empathy and experience with their problem. For example, runners prefer to take their injuries to runner-friendly doctors. Even though the recommendation may be to stop running and start swimming, most runners take such advice more seriously if given by a doctor who also runs versus a doctor who has never experienced the pleasures of running. Just a detail or two about yourself in the context of your client's dilemma can inspire a trusting relationship. Your client then sees that you relate to his problem and, since you have also experienced a similar predicament, will probably have much more to offer him. Your client feels connected to the process of solving the problem, rather than manipulated by some specialist who lectures with a memorized list of shoulds and shouldn'ts.

Your intent is not to steal the show and become the center of attention. Instead, you want to connect with your client's experience in order to influence a positive outcome. It is the customer's movie that takes priority here, so unless you can shift your focus to the speaker's movie and steer clear of your own, sharing information about yourself is not advised. Many of us have had the experience of paying a consultant big bucks only to have most of the session taken up by the consultant's monologue about his own problems.

Some of the most effective therapists, doctors, and salespeople I have known are those who focus on connecting with their clients. Their good results with patients and customers stem from their ability to use the movie mindset. Jack Carew, a well-known sales trainer and author of *The Mentor: 15 Ways to Success in Sales, Business and Life*, supports the movie mindset as a way to understand the speaker. Only through understanding does a salesperson have the power to influence a customer:

You really don't discover what the customer wants until you deliberately listen to him. . . . If you don't really understand what's important to the customer, preparing your sales proposal will be as futile as mowing your lawn at midnight. You will not know where you've been or where you are going. You will be inviting stiff resistance to your solution because you didn't give the customer a role in helping you discover the problem. Only when you understand your customer's needs will you be in a position to resolve the customer's problem and ultimately win the business. . . . You will get and hold your customer's interest in you by staying in his operating reality or area of interest.

You have all heard about getting into the shoes of the speaker, but getting into his movie is a more powerful mental shift: you are not trying merely to see into the personality of the speaker, but rather the circumstances and motivations that make that person tick. A mediator friend told me about a concept in conflict management called *attribution* and the way it interferes with resolving conflict. We tend to justify our shortcomings, such as tardiness or disorganization, as the result of environmental conditions. We are late because the train was late; we are disorganized today because we have a new secretary. Yet when someone else is late for a meeting or appears disorganized, we do not take into account the possible mishaps she may have encountered that day. Instead, we attribute her lateness to a personality flaw—"She's lazy" or "He's not reliable." Getting into the movie helps you to be less critical and realize that circumstances beyond our control can occur to anyone at any time.

One of my best experiences in witnessing the power of the movie mindset was in graduate school. A very experienced speech pathologist and researcher, Dr. Blom, at the Indianapolis Medical Center, was counseling a patient who had had his voice box removed due to cancer. Dr. Blom encouraged the man to try a voice restoration device so that he could communicate easier on the job. The patient was a sixty-eight-year-old farmer from a small town in Indiana. It was only his second time in twenty-six years in a big city; the first time had been his surgery two weeks earlier. It was obvious that the man was feeling low. He was unable to speak (except with the aid of an electronic device called an electrolarynx), and he was quite anxious about having to deal with yet another medical procedure. His well-weathered overalls, ruddy complexion, and callused fingers stood out in stark contrast with the gleaming, sterile background of the examination room.

The patient sat rigidly in his chair, nervously awaiting his examination and—most probably—a painful procedure. Sensing the farmer's nervousness and apprehension, Dr. Blom put down his instruments and pulled up a chair across from the patient. He had noticed a tiny ornament in the shape of a fishing hook pinned to the farmer's overalls. Dr. Blom sat back in his chair and asked him about the pin. The farmer started talking about fishing in nearby Lake Munroe. He visibly relaxed as he began, using his electronic voice, to share a fishing story. The farmer's eyes lit up as he relived the day he hooked the biggest bluefish ever caught in the county!

Everyone in the room, including those of us who had never gone fishing in our lives, were glued to their seats. For about ten minutes, he told us about the joys of fishing in Indiana. Then, with a big smile on his face and tears in his eyes, he thanked us for listening. Then he turned to Dr. Blom and said, "Let's see if that fancy gadget works!" With a willing and relaxed patient, Dr. Blom carried out the necessary procedure in less than five minutes. The farmer left, relieved and satisfied, with the sense that he had just made a friend.

Applying the movie mindset when listening opportunities arise teaches us to be sensitive to the speaker's needs and feelings. Even though the farmer's words denied fear and nervousness, the doctor sensed his worry and chose to be sensitive to his client's needs. Dr.

Blom knew that if he exposed his patient's apprehension directly, the farmer would have been embarrassed and ultimately resentful.

By forgetting about yourself for a few minutes, you glimpse how your speaker feels about his situation. He may not come out and say, "I feel so frustrated right now," or "I'm very pleased with your service," but because the movie mindset takes you to a level of communication that is deeper than words, you can get a pretty good sense of his view of the situation. The speaker's views may shock, embarrass, aggravate, or hurt you, but you have been truthful with yourself in accepting the existence of another's reality. As a mindful listener, you strive to relate to the needs—positive or negative—of the speaker. This is reflected in words, body language, and tone of voice. If this seems difficult, try to imagine how you would like people to respond to you in a similar situation. (I will delve more into self-listening in chapters seven and eight.)

Before you picked up this book you may have approached your daily conversation partners as one-dimensional characters, merely talking heads with different hairdos. As you learned in chapter three, part of the reason we have such difficulties remembering what was said is that our barriers distance us from the speaker. We may hear the words, but not fully understand or let ourselves accept the meaning behind the words. Your friend, for example, may tell you about her problems with her new boss, yet you are not aware of how serious her concerns are unless you share her movie.

Let's say your vice-president stops you in the hall to discuss a new project. Instead of processing the key ideas in order to make a mental record for the upcoming meeting, you focus instead on a negative experience you had on a past project. By letting that past experience snatch your attention, you set yourself apart and remain outside the theater, so to speak. Failed business and social relationships and lost opportunities result from letting our barriers distance us from the speaker and his views. Instead, when you encounter a situation in which you need to listen well, ask yourself, "What's his movie? What's her reality? How does he see things right now?" This gives you a window into that person's world and a chance to give your own agenda a rest. When you are absorbed in the speaker's movie, not only do his words take on a deeper meaning, but even his gestures and facial expressions add another layer to your understanding.

According to Albert Mehrabian, author of *Silent Messages,* the listener perceives 55 percent of the meaning of the spoken message through gestures and facial expressions; 38 percent is interpreted through tone of voice, speech rate, rhythm, and emphasis; and words transmit approximately 7 percent of the message. In other words, nonverbal cues communicate the bulk of the message. This supports the notion that indeed actions speak louder than words. Yet it is up to the listener to synthesize words, actions, and vocal cues to arrive at the whole message the speaker intends to convey. The movie mindset facilitates this synthesis.

Richard Ben Cramer, in his book *What It Takes,* compares communication styles of various presidential candidates. He speaks highly of Senator Richard Gephardt's ability to get into the movie of the speaker:

> When Gephardt started to listen, his whole person went into receive mode. He locked his sky-blue eyes on your face, and they didn't wiggle around between your eyes and your mouth and the guy who walked in the door behind you, they were just on you, still and absorptive, like a couple of small blotters. . . . If it was just you and your problem, he'd stay on receive until you were weak from being listened to.

Our powerful self-interests set limits on what we permit ourselves to experience. Why not turn those self interests into an interested self? Mahatma Gandhi described the rewards of getting into the speaker's movie when he said, "Three-fourths of the miseries and misunderstandings in the world will disappear if we step in the shoes of our adversaries and understand their viewpoint."

The movie mindset confers the gift of another's vision of life. Everyone's movie is an adventure. Granted, some movies may not be as adventurous as others, but at least if you give the speaker a chance, you run the risk only of learning something new.

Another benefit of getting into someone else's movie is how good it makes the speaker feel. Can you recall the exuberance you felt the last time you had a captive audience? Telling that story or joke was like experiencing it for the first time—even *you* became immersed in the plot again. The audience were willing hostages, bound to your experience. You also know the lonely feeling of inviting someone to share your movie and getting no response, or worse, hearing that person belittle or devalue your experience. When that happens, it's easy to let negative self-talk intervene and convince you that your experience wasn't that great after all. You can see how not truly being heard can affect self-esteem.

I frequently ask students, "When you are the speaker, how do you know that you have been heard?" The majority say that they feel they have been heard when their concerns become the concerns of the listener, when their needs or feelings have been understood or interpreted correctly, and when the listener responds appropriately. Other responses include:

- When they don't keep asking me the same questions.

- When they look at me and do nothing else while I speak.

- When they don't start talking about themselves or something totally different.

- When I see them days or weeks later and they ask about something I said days or weeks ago, as though it was important enough to stay on their minds.

- When they act on what I said.

When I ask, "How do you feel when you have been listened to?", responses are quite varied:

- A feeling of relief.

- Guilty, like I'm dumping on them.

- That my opinion counts.

- Like someone cares about me and my point of view.

- Appreciative and a little guilty for feeling so good afterward.

- It makes me feel important.

By getting into the movie of your speakers, you not only benefit in the sense of understanding them better, but, as you can see from the responses, speakers feel respected, even apologetic for taking your time.

I find the guilty reaction difficult to explain, except that perhaps because there are so few moments in our lives when we are truly heard, it is like receiving a rare gift for which we can offer no equal. Listening is a very inexpensive way to give to others. It is unfortunate that we feel the need to give money or material things to make others feel valued. Several studies have shown that workers prefer nonmaterial reinforcement and recognition for a job well done rather than money. Truly listening, forgetting yourself for a short time, and getting into the speaker's movie can be the kindest gift you can give to another. It is emotionally uplifting to speak to a person instead of a wall or a TV. As the listener, it doesn't matter if you cannot offer the solution to the problem; at least you can be the sounding board, which is frequently all it takes for the speaker to determine her own solution. As speakers, we develop the trust of mindful listeners and look forward to interacting with them again.

Trust does not develop when the other party merely acts like he is listening. A study by Ramsey and Sohi in 1997 shows that ". . . when customers feel that a salesperson is listening to what they are saying, it enhances their trust in that salesperson." The results also show that when customers feel that a salesperson is honest and sincere they are likely to be satisfied in their dealings with him or her. Similarly, trust in the salesperson increases customers' anticipation of future interaction with that salesperson.

Isn't this the same trust you want to build with your spouse, children, and friends? The movie mindset is a shift to the reality of the speaker, not a list of dos and don'ts or tricks to demonstrate that you are listening. Your aim is not to make speakers perceive you as working hard to listen. False listening is worse than no listening at all. The harder you work at listening, at getting people to like you, to meet your customer quota, or make money, the more you work against yourself. It's like golf. The harder you try to hit the ball, the greater the chance that you'll miss it. The movie mindset is the path of less resistance to achieving the success that comes from good listening. This is because your aim is simply to understand the speaker. Everything else falls into place if you get into the speaker's movie.

Coincidentally, the movie experience gradually results in other needed changes in your communication behavior. You begin to find *your* movies less pressing, and therefore you are less prone to talk so much about yourself. Your movie, despite a great story line, gets to be boring, and you learn nothing from playing it over and over again.

As I apply the movie mindset to listening situations, I have become more reluctant to talk about myself and my knowledge of a subject. I am happy to share what I know, but I would much rather delve into another's scenery and get a fresh perspective. Forgetting yourself and getting into the speaker's movie is like going on a vacation from your ego.

One of my students described his experience using the movie mindset:

> Every customer takes me on a journey to his land of problems and concerns. If I let myself become preoccupied with my problems and concerns while listening to his, my day turns out to be a drain on my energy. If, on the other hand, I enter into his situation and forget myself, my day turns into a Technicolor experience! My customers seem less difficult to deal with, I get the job done, and I go home at night telling my wife stories about my fascinating clients. I see my job now in a very different light. I look forward to each workday as a new adventure. Who would ever think that the job of a repo man would be an enlightening experience?

Another plus to the movie frame of mind, just like at the movies, is that except for an occasional exclamation, our tendency to interrupt significantly decreases. Speakers rate interrupting as the number-one most annoying conversational trait. Wanting to interrupt is a struggle for power in conversation. If you are an interrupter, notice how attached you are to controlling the topic and getting across your point of view, how immersed you are in *your* movie, how you are distancing yourself from the listener. (There will be more about interrupting in chapter 8.)

The more you practice getting into other people's movies, the more you will notice how much better people respond to you. We all appreciate a nonjudgmental ear. When listening in the movie, our barriers do not interfere. Because we are seeing from the speaker's perspective, we are not in a position to judge. Instead, the motivation of the speaker's actions are revealed to us. In the end, we may agree or disagree with her views, but we have allowed ourselves to understand why our speaker feels the way she does. In turn, speakers will naturally want to hear from you. You can only hope that when it is your turn to talk, you can contribute to your listeners' knowledge in a worthwhile way.

There are some situations in which getting too deeply immersed in another's movie is not advisable. Doctors working in a emergency room in a big city hospital, for example, may find the movie mindset exhausting and unproductive. Emotions continually run high and many patients' movies are of epic proportions. In a life-or-death situation, listening to how the patient ended up in the ER is not a priority. A physician needs to act quickly and maintain concentration in order to save lives. Yet a social worker, a lawyer, or a policeman may find it necessary to get into the movie of the victim to take the appropriate legal action.

For patients and their families, it is necessary for the physician and staff to acknowledge their feelings and help them find a way to cope. I tip my hat to the physician who, faced with a critically ill patient, can walk that tightrope between sharing the patient's feelings and preserving the necessary objectivity to see that patient and his family through treatment.

Crisis counselors who offer telephone support to the distressed and potentially suicidal are at high risk for burnout. For purposes of safety and openness, these sainted volunteers can offer only phone support and must remain anonymous. Due to the magnitude of callers' difficulties, sometimes these discussions can go on for an hour or more. In addition, counselors have to choose their words carefully and are frequently subjected to harassment or manipulation by the caller. To become too deeply entrenched in the emotional problems of these needy persons puts a counselor at risk for not being able to offer constructive advice in a time of crisis.

Listening to a stroke patient trying to communicate with one good hand, a myriad of facial expressions, and incomprehensible words is a particular challenge. You have to focus on finding the patient's intent and facilitate the release of his thought through some medium—a picture board, spellboard, or writing. This requires you to feel and try to imagine what could be on his mind. Most times, it is neither a bedpan nor a blanket that the patient wants. Instead, it may be his need to hear that his frozen speech is only temporary. Unhappily, this prognosis is not always the case. Equally difficult is dealing with family members who cannot communicate with a loved one victimized by a stroke or head injury. In these situations, distance is not required, and the movie mindset can help you try to understand their pain. It is a way of lightening their burden. They do not need you to cry with them; they need you to listen as they voice their fears and remorse. Only then can they discuss treatment alternatives and make rational decisions about rehabilitative strategies. If patients and families are not genuinely heard during these difficult times, their ability to cope with their situation and accept help will be greatly compromised.

Those of you who complain about poor attention span will probably say that you rarely have a problem concentrating at the movies. In a movie theater there are no other distractions. It is dark and you are so involved with what's happening on the screen that you don't even pay attention to the strangers sitting only inches away to the left and right. Your ability to concentrate is magnificent! However, it is the everyday stuff, like meetings and lectures, that challenge your ability to concentrate.

Most of us have had the experience of becoming absorbed in a movie, so we know how it feels. It is not something we have to *learn* how to do. Yet why is it difficult to get into a conversation partner's movie?

Perhaps the problem lies in your ability to connect with the speaker. How can you step out of your reality and into another's if you have deeper self-concerns competing for attention? Getting out of your own movie and becoming a mindful listener requires three things: 1) the desire to get the whole message, 2) the ability to eliminate the noisy barriers discussed in chapter two, and 3) the willingness to place your agenda lower on the priority list. A mindful listener is not a jealous listener. For example, when a friend or coworker returns from vacation exuberant about his adventures, do you wonder resentfully where he got the money or ruminate on how you wish you had gone somewhere equally exciting? As if there are only a finite number of good vacations to be had or a limited number of promotions to be earned, you may not feel compelled to lend a generous ear. Would you then be satisfied if you could hoard all the great experiences that exist?

On the other hand, if your conversation partner is just plain boring you—like a bad movie—it's a challenge to look for the golden nugget of information or opportunity. You will not find it shuffling along with your eyes focused on the horizon. (Chapter ten will be helpful with these more challenging listening conditions.)

Opening your mind to another's point of view may make you uncomfortable, but your willingness to bend by putting yourself aside to get into your partner's movie is a powerful force in forming stable marital relationships. John Gottman, a psychology professor and marriage-therapy guru at the University of Washington, claims that "only those newlywed men who are accepting of influence from their wives are winding up in happy, stable marriages." He goes on to say that by "getting husbands to share power with their wives by accepting some of the demands they make is critical in helping to resolve conflict." This new approach to marriage counseling may prove more effective than the traditional method of teaching couples mechanical listening approaches like active listening.

Let's examine another path to learning more about our nature. According to Abraham Maslow, the eminent psychologist, the goal of self-development is to achieve self-actualization. If you are self-actualized, you are eager to reach a level of understanding that eventually frees you from focusing on yourself and allows you to focus on others instead. You lack self-consciousness and are psychologically free to explore others' insights. You can turn everyday routines into peak experiences. Each conversation can be as exhilarating as standing breathless before a magnificent sunrise or reveling in the warmth and scent of a crackling hearth on a frigid afternoon.

Eleanor Roosevelt and Henry David Thoreau were among the people Maslow characterized as self-actualized. They accepted themselves and others for what they were. They did not wait for the approval of others before taking action. Self-actualizers listen as though no one else on earth exists at that moment. Isn't that how you want your customers, friends, and family to feel after speaking to you?

Getting into someone else's movie is a natural way of listening. There is no step-by-step approach, nor is it contrived. It is an extension of your curiosity about what it's like to be in their shoes. As a result, people respond to you better because they notice that you are less judgmental and less critical. Dr. Maslow says, "The most efficient way to perceive the intrinsic nature of the world is to be more receptive than active."

Where are you on the road to self-actualization? How secure is your foundation for *listening readiness?* According to Maslow's hierarchy of needs, there are four levels of needs to be satisfied before you are ready to seek self-actualization. The order of needs described below is not fixed, and may vary among individuals. The degree of satisfaction may also differ.

Level 1 involves the basic physiological needs, such as hunger, thirst, sex, and sleep. Once these needs are met, a new set of needs emerges. Level 2 requires a sense of safety. If you have not satisfied your needs at this level, you will mistrust others and be overly cautious in new situations. Next come the needs for affection from others and feeling like part of a group. Maslow refers to these needs as *love* and *belongingness*. Level 4 includes the desire for self-esteem and the ability to achieve goals, to be independent and competent. You are then said to be growth oriented, extending beyond yourself and your ego to become receptive to a wide vista of perception. A self-actualized person becomes, in essence, receptive to seeing life from someone else's perspective.

How to satisfy your basic needs toward becoming self-actualized is beyond the scope of this book, but if you are having difficulty letting yourself listen or if you find it difficult to work through your barriers, there may be other unmet personal needs that require attention and perhaps professional counseling. Attending to some of your unmet basic needs and working your way up the ladder, you can look forward to listening becoming a peak experience.

When you routinely substitute artificial means of communication (e-mail, Internet chat rooms, form letters), you reduce your opportunities for peak experiences that can change your life. Perhaps the attraction of these media is to establish the connections we crave without the hassles of face-to-face contact. Occasionally, my students complain about the inefficiency and dissatisfaction they experience with direct contact with family, friends, or customers. According to them, people don't say what's on their minds; they act foolishly, laugh too much, and beat around the bush. They interrupt, judge, give unrequested advice, and talk too much.

Being drawn into an interesting movie is a spontaneous experience; you do not have to work hard to listen or rely on technique to get into the character's shoes. It is only when we block the spontaneity of listening by focusing on outcome rather than process that listening becomes stilted. Posing, head nodding, and other mechanical listening tricks are unnatural and actually interfere with listening. In *The Way of Zen,* Alan Watts illustrates the virtues of unself-conscious action by describing a centipede's skill in using a hundred legs at once:

> The centipede was happy, quite
> Until a toad in fun
> said, "Pray, which leg goes after which?"
> This worked his mind to such a pitch,
> He lay distracted in a ditch
> Considering how to run.

One of the most interesting listening situations I ever experienced was with my Russian mother-in-law a few summers ago. Unable to speak more than five words of English (four of them dealt with shopping), Etel came to Boston for a visit. My Russian, limited to very basic conversation, contributed nothing but small talk to our relationship. Fortunately, my husband, fluent in English and Russian, was usually around to help with the translation. One night, however, he had to go to a meeting. Earlier in the day he had told me that Etel was tired of watching American TV and preferred to spend the evening talking with me. How, I asked, could she possibly find my limited Russian more entertaining than *Wheel of Fortune?* I pleaded with him to reschedule his meeting! Alas, there was no way out.

After my husband left, I boldly brought out tea and cookies, a Russian dictionary tucked discreetly under my arm, while Etel sat patiently at the dining room table. This, I thought, is going to be the Russian crash course from hell. I poured the tea, hoping that the grammar rules would kick in sometime within the next couple of hours. Etel smiled and looked at me as though I were an old friend and began talking slowly. From the few words and names I could pick up, I deduced that she was talking about life in the old Soviet Union. Gradually, she began to pick up speed, and she became somewhat melancholy. Although I could barely pick out a familiar word, it was obvious that Etel was reliving the past and having a great time telling me about it.

Etel did not sense that I was lost. How could she keep talking without checking to see if I was following her story? At that point, I could have stopped trying and merely nodded every so often to be polite. But I decided to persist. If I couldn't understand her words, I could still listen to the expression in her voice and watch her face. I could also have switched to an overly active approach to listening, interrupting to look up unfamiliar words, asking for repetitions, but I knew instinctively that was not what my mother-in-law needed at the time. Etel needed me to just *listen*. I stayed vigilant; if I surrendered my attention for even a moment, I would lose what fragments of the message I had understood.

An hour went by and I was right there with her *as the KGB officer searched her belongings looking for black-market goods. He reached deep into the side pockets where she had hidden the American blue jeans and the Beatles tapes she had purchased for her son! As she broke out in a cold sweat, the officer glanced up, first with a glare and then with a wink, shut her suitcase and let her go!*

Later, I began to think that my interpretation of what Etel said was off the mark, but it didn't matter—Etel was having the time of her life! My ego, initially obsessed with getting every word and verb tense correct, decided to take an aisle seat and enjoy the show.

An hour later when my husband finally came home, I was sorry to see these stories come to an end. Prior to this night, I had never seen Etel laugh out loud or show so much emotion. I'll probably never know the real stories she shared, but that night changed our relationship. Listening to her did more to establish closeness between us than a hundred shopping trips.

Let's go to the movies

1. Go to the movies or rent a video if you don't have too many distractions at home. An action film or thriller increases your chances of getting involved. Notice how caught up you become and how your body language reflects your involvement in the drama. (I'll bet you didn't plan to lean forward, eyes glued to the screen, when the spy whispers the secret code to his lover prior to falling into shark-infested waters!) Also notice how, during the less exciting parts, your mind wanders and how often you have to remind yourself to *get back into the movie.* Are you able to follow the plot or do you easily get lost? Think about how often you drift in and out of conversations and miss out on the plot or the main ideas. Some TV talk shows and sitcoms also lend themselves to this exercise. Using movies or TV shows to sharpen your ability to concentrate is effortless and enjoyable. Afterward, you can reflect on how you were able to put aside your to-do list and forget your own agenda for a while.

2. Plan to get into at least one person's movie a day. It could be a client, a child, or the person who cleans your office. Look forward to a great miniadventure! It might be the cab driver telling you about her busy day, a coworker describing his weekend, or a child relating a funny thing that happened in school. *Live it with them—just like in the movies.* Experience the sensation of being in two places at once—in your chair *and* in the speaker's situation. Notice how time stops.

3. Cultural differences pose special challenges to even the best listeners. To get into the movies of people from other countries, you need to be somewhat knowledgeable of their culture and how they feel comfortable relating to others. If your new job or community is made up of foreign-born people, find some literature on their social customs. Pay attention to the kinds of questions, comments, or nonverbal clues that are unique to them. It even makes good business sense to study these differences. Remember, a good listener seeks to understand the speaker.

4. Next, you need to apply this listening mindset to less thrilling but more realistic settings like lectures or meetings. Each speaker has a movie to share. Choose an audiocassette or a radio talk show (like public radio) with few interruptions to practice your concentration powers. Notice how many of the main points you were able to remember. What was the golden nugget of that interview about quantum mechanics? If the topic was not of particular interest, perhaps it was the way the speaker argued his point and handled the criticisms of the interviewer. Go for the gold during these listening opportunities; there's always *something* to be gained. But please, don't get too involved in the debate when you are driving—you may miss your exit!

Chapter Six

Mindfulness: Listening in the Moment

If you cannot find the truth where you are,
Where do you expect to find it?

—Master Dogen

In my search for a decent pair of ski pants in a perfectly yuppie ski store, my attention was momentarily snatched by a video advertisement for upscale ski gear. There I was, surfing the racks of jackets and pants, and suddenly the whoosh of skis and a beguiling male chuckle stole my glance. On a large TV monitor was a mountain climber scaling a jagged wall of sunlit ice. The next shot showed a skier being dropped from a helicopter into a powdery bed of snow high above a no-name mountain range (it had to be the Himalayas, I thought!). The sights were spectacular and the athletes courageous, and it was all designed to make the average person like me feel like we were missing out on something—big time.

In between these breath-taking escapades flashed the words that made me sad for those who would take them to heart: "I am not alive when I'm in the office . . . I am not alive when I'm in a taxi . . ." This was clearly code for *I feel alive only when I'm doing something exciting, like risking my life.* Our innate power to stay focused in the present moment, no matter what the task, lies smoldering under the ashes of wishing and dreaming to be anywhere else except where we are right now.

This experience made me think about how extremes of preference and denying the worth of our daily activities and the people in them, for that matter, set us up to feel depressed, stressed, and resentful. For example, cafeteria talk abounds with the following sentiments: *Work is a drag. . . . I live for the weekend. . . . Is it Friday yet? . . . I hate Mondays. . . . It's just a job. . . .* We spend so much energy and thought hardwiring these preferences into our brains that there is little room for seeing our work or our weekends any other way.

The Zen masters claim that it is this constant judgment of people and things, plus our critical self-judgments, that bring on suffering. The barriers to listening discussed in chapter four are some of the ways that we punish ourselves every day. Since we are so attached to our weekends, we rush through work in order to get out of work. We make mistakes, scrimp on quality, and feel guilty, knowing we could have done better. Attachment to these barriers stifles creativity and limits our receptivity to new ideas. Furthermore, this internal strife breeds distractibility and discontent, which in turn weaken concentration and memory. It will take a mighty big raise or a catastrophic event to see our work in another light.

So it is with listening to others. Either the speaker's comments jibe with our way of seeing the world or they do not. Judging and attacking ideas that are contrary to our frame of reference is a form of suffering. It is energy depleting, both internally (makes you frustrated and tense) and externally (creates tension between you and the speaker). The result is poor relationships with others, lost opportunities, and low self-esteem, which are the *real* suffering.

In previous chapters I have described meditation—watching

the breath—as the most natural and effective way to calm the cacophony of the mind. Improved concentration allows you to connect better with the task at hand, regardless of its desirable or undesirable qualities, by producing a deep state of calm accompanied (over time) by a broader and more balanced view of everyday tasks. You see the different features of a task as interdependent and complementary. You may still have preferences, but they remain flexible in your mind—you become less fearful of change.

This more balanced attitude relates directly to listening. If you recall from chapter two, the working definition of mindful listening includes the ability to sustain attention to the spoken word over time. Your ability to concentrate on the message allows you to process and retain the information and determines how well you will remember it minutes and years later.

Concentration is the key to performing *any* meaningful activity well. It is heartening to know that we innately possess the ability to concentrate. It does not require any special training, just frequent application. Think of an activity that requires complete, sustained attention, such as taking an important test, driving in a snowstorm, or playing chess. Your focus on these tasks is propelled by a strong intent to assure a positive outcome—to excel in school, get home safely, or choose the best move. However, the more you concentrate on the *process*, the more positive will be the outcome. Reading each test item carefully, looking for tricky wordings, and rechecking your answers increases your chance of scoring a high grade. If you were to think of nothing but getting an A, the end result would not be so positive.

On the other hand, there are activities that once required a similar level of concentration, but have now become mindless, like sweeping the floor or grocery shopping. These rote activities give the brain a chance to unwind and relax. You can think about other things and even perform other tasks simultaneously: you can eat *and* read, surf the Internet *and* listen to music. These combinations can be very enjoyable. However, you may tend to overuse this ability to multitask and misuse it when it is necessary to focus your attention on a single activity, such as listening. Our environment with its constant bombardment of stimuli challenges your innate ability to relax and focus completely on one task at a time.

Not long ago, I was in an airport with an hour wait for my plane, and I met a former high-school classmate whom I hadn't seen in more than twenty years. We decided to go across the street to a nice hotel for something to drink while we caught up on each other's lives. Outside the bar was a sign that invited us to COME IN AND RELAX. As soon as we were inside, we noticed five TVs, all tuned to different channels! In addition, there was noise from the nearby kitchen and a radio playing behind the bar. Some patrons at tables tried to maintain conversation-like activities while their eyes shifted from TV to TV. It was dizzying! It took every bit of our concentration to hear each other and even more effort to discuss anything in depth. It occurred to me that an intensely distracting environment is regarded by many people as "relaxing."

You lull yourself into a false sense of competency when you think you can make dinner, plan that sales meeting, and help your son with his homework, all at the same time. You may finish all these tasks in thirty minutes or less, but how is the quality? When you look closely, dinner was just edible, you overlooked two of the seven main points for the meeting, and your son is able to spell only six of the ten words on his vocabulary homework. Since the goal is to *finish* these tasks so that you can rush onto the next one, the results are less than satisfactory. You feel depleted and inadequate.

Such mindlessness becomes a habit and begins to creep into tasks that require your full concentration. How often do you look back at the week, the month, the year, and wonder where the time went? Many of us can't remember because most of the time we were in a fog of preoccupation with the past or planning the future. Our attention was scattered all over the place, and the quality of our actions was just good enough to get by. Substandard performance on any task results in low self-esteem and lack of fulfillment.

Eknath Easwaran, author of *Words to Live By: Inspiration for Every Day,* speaks of the dangers of mindlessness: "There is no joy in work which is hurried, which is done when we are at the mercy of pressures from outside, because such work is compulsive. All too often hurry clouds judgment. More and more, to save time, a person tends to think in terms of pat solutions and to take shortcuts and give uninspired performances."

When mindlessness teams up with personal barriers, our ability to concentrate on the message is out of reach. The antidote is to challenge those distractions and focus on the process—establishing a warm relationship with another person, seeing the other's view, and accepting it as valid whether you agree with it or not. Focus on process ensures the favorable outcome you hope for—repeat sales, cooperation from difficult people, better recall. When you listen in a state of mindfulness, your thinking does not yield to the negative barriers described in chapter four. If, however, you still find that your barriers overpower your ability to focus, then you need to spend a bit more time thinking them through.

In my search for a practical means of improving the ability to concentrate and listen more effectively, I came across the writings of Thich Nhat Hanh, a Zen Buddhist monk. After studying his book, *The Miracle of Mindfulness,* I found that my ability to listen had become richer. The essence of Zen is to be in the present. Thich Nhat Hanh describes mindfulness as keeping your consciousness alive to the present reality. Living the present moment of any activity, paying attention to the process, lend themselves to a quality outcome.

A good way to experience mindfulness is to choose a task you typically rush through, like washing the dishes. According to Thich

Nhat Hanh, "There are two ways to wash the dishes. The first is to wash the dishes in order to have clean dishes and the second is to wash the dishes in order to wash the dishes." He says that if we hurry through the dishes, thinking only about the cup of tea that awaits us, then we are not washing the dishes to wash the dishes; we are not alive during the time we are washing the dishes. In fact, we are completely incapable of realizing the miracle of life while standing at the sink. "If we can't wash the dishes," he continues, "the chances are we won't be able to drink our tea either. While drinking the cup of tea, we will only be thinking of other things, barely aware of the cup in our hands."

When you are listening to another but planning your own agenda at the same time, you are really talking to yourself and therefore not truly listening. You have escaped the present in order to be in the future. You may be physically present, but mentally you are bouncing back and forth between past events and future expectations.

Another challenge to mindful listening is that the average person speaks at a rate of 125 words per minute, yet we can process up to 500 words per minute. During that lag time, you can think about your to-do list or you can listen mindfully by using that time to summarize what the speaker has said so far or see the possibilities in what the speaker is proposing. You can also note the emphasis in his voice or the degree of concern in his gestures and facial expressions. When you are in the speaker's movie, you use your resources to be a competent, intelligent listener.

If you have difficulty putting your thoughts, judgments, and other noise aside while you are trying to get into the speaker's movie, you may need some practice staying in the present. Poor listeners have little patience for the present. Thoughts of yesterday and tomorrow are more enticing. Your barriers have little tolerance for information or ideas that are contrary or too lengthy. Impatience shows itself when you fall out of the speaker's movie or want to interrupt.

This is where your daily meditation practice can help. Watching the breath for twenty minutes or more, once or twice a day, is the most effective way to cultivate a sense of comfort with the present. During your practice, do not work at avoiding thoughts of past and future; this is impatience creeping in. Simply recognize the presence of those thoughts and let them pass. Gently steer your focus back to the breath, back to the present. Feel and listen to your breath as it moves in and out. After a while you can breathe less consciously, and eventually you will be able to step back and let the breath move on its own. The same automatic focus will persist when listening. You will be able to step back from your barriers and, without much work, take in the whole message.

Time spent listening, consulting, teaching, or working in the present can be just as memorable as those moments in your life when time appeared to stand still. When listening mindfully, however, your perception is heightened and you experience multilevel awareness. You are able to delve into what makes the speaker tick, how well his body language matches or contradicts his spoken message, his mood, energy level, and other subtle nuances. When you are fully absorbed in the speaker's movie, you are in the present; time appears to stand still. Mindful listening is not a trance or a hypnotic state. You are aware of your surroundings, but they are not a distraction.

The first-century Buddhist philosopher Ashvagosha gives a humorous account of mindful listening:

> If we are listening to a friend, even if a parrot flies down and perches on his head, we should not get excited, point to the parrot, and burst out, "Excuse me for interrupting, but there's a parrot on your head." We should be able to concentrate so hard on what our friend is saying that we can tell this urge, "Keep quiet and don't distract me. Afterwards I'll tell him about the bird."

He goes on to describe mindfulness as "one-pointedness." This means to focus the attention completely on one task at a time. By applying this approach to your daily tasks, you can complete the same number of tasks, only with better quality, and hence, better outcomes. Many of my students tell me they are better able to prioritize activities and eliminate the time wasters. When being mindful appears daunting, remember that one minute of mindfulness makes up for many minutes of mindlessness.

My first experience with mindful listening came on the wings of a martial arts class a few years ago. (Whenever I share this story in my class, there are always a few students who have also studied martial arts who will smile and nod their heads.) In my first martial arts class, after a short breathing meditation, my instructor demonstrated a series of three movements for me to practice by myself. He assigned me to a corner of the room and turned his attention to the higher belts. I couldn't help but notice the black-belt student only inches from my space whirling, with what appeared to be complete control, a jong bong (a six-foot wooden stick). In front of me were a couple of students practicing knife defenses. The instructor noticed my lapses of concentration as I repeated the three-step exercise. After a few reminders, I was punished with a series of fifty pushups that quickly helped me to focus. Never, since grade school, was I so humiliated and humbled by having a weakness exposed publicly. With every class my concentration improved, but not because of the threat of fifty pushups. Rather, it was the sheer pleasure of feeling focused and centered on my task, which was to carry out each movement to the best of my understanding. Eventually, I went beyond what I thought to be my physical limits. What I had always blamed on poor coordination turned out to be the fault of poor concentration and delinquent listening.

Through three years of tears and tests, the mind-body connection began to seem attainable. Mindfulness would stay with me longer and longer after each class, at first just until I reached my doorstep, then for days and ultimately weeks. My work and my personal life reflected this conscientiousness. Even cleaning the martial arts studio after each class along with the other students (originally I judged this as degrading) gave me a sense of contributing to the well-being of my fellow students and the school. After awhile, I noticed it was the higher belts who offered to clean the toilets and scrub the corners. No task was too menial; every task was completed with concentration and care. Now I could better understand how the monks in a monastery take special joy in repeating the same chores day after day.

A similar mind-body connection was described by Mihaly Czikszentmihalyi, author of *Flow*. He defines a flow experience as the pleasant state of concentration or total absorption in a task. Those he interviewed—painters, dancers, and athletes—said that when they were in the midst of their art or hobby, their state of focused energy was like "floating" or "being carried by the flow." When you experience flow often, the quality of your life improves. The opposite of flow is mindlessness. During mindless listening, your barriers create resistance to the message; your mind is scattered.

During my most gratifying listening moments, when my interest and concern about what someone is saying overwhelm my barriers, the sense of flow or timelessness is striking. Sometimes, running with my predawn companions, for example, I become so involved in what my friend says that I don't become breathless climbing a steep incline, nor do I care that it is only ten degrees outside. The run is effortless, and I feel smooth and light and extremely happy.

Take a minute to think of times when you have experienced being in the flow of an activity. It may have been as simple as frosting a cake or as complex as solving a quantum physics equation. How can we summon that sense of flow as we listen to someone?

In my listening classes, we begin to practice mindfulness in gentler doses. We begin by experiencing orange juice as I narrate. Students watch the rush of the deep orange color as the juice is poured into their cups. Together, we smell the citrus perfume and notice how our mouths begin to water. We sip and savor the tartness. We consider the work that went into producing this cup of juice and imagine the beauty of the tree from which it came. We think about the people who made it possible to get the juice to our table. This full experience endures until the last sip. As they listen and ponder the juice, it's always interesting to note that no one looks around the room; each one's gaze and mental focus are centered on the juice.

The point of the exercise is to take a simple human act, something that we typically take for granted, and make it come alive. So often we sleep through life, attributing little or no meaning to our daily activities. Imagine if you lent that same zest to sipping your coffee, conducting a meeting, or cleaning out the refrigerator; how much more satisfied would you feel at the end of the day? I can be sure my students will never again drink orange juice the old way. And if they need a mindfulness refresher, they will simply pour themselves a glass of orange juice.

Mindfulness connects us with the experience of the moment, no matter what the activity. With listening, mindfulness connects us to the listener. *Mindlessness*, on the other hand, means letting the ego-dominated self—concerns with status, past experiences, and other barriers—separate us from the listener. The mindful listener lacks this obsessive self-consciousness that interferes with the ability to concentrate. We feel happier and more positive when we are not focusing on the self.

The most direct way to improve your concentration and become mindful of the present is to practice daily meditation. Meditation helps you to experience a sense of here-and-nowness so that it becomes easier to transfer that state to the act of listening. Quiet, undisturbed deep breathing instills a sense of calm that is conducive to focus. Those who practice meditation know that after even a few days, the ability to stay focused is noticeable. Simply stated, if you cannot keep your mind centered on your breath, how can you expect to concentrate effectively on anything else?

Regular meditation practice has a way of neutralizing your personal prejudices and negative self-talk. These barriers may still pop up from time to time, but they become easier to set aside and impinge less upon your ability to listen selflessly. Because your mind is free of self-conscious noise, you have space to make room for the concerns of others. This is where compassionate or empathetic listening begins.

When you are calm, you can eliminate the noise and pay attention to many different layers of the message simultaneously. Just as a wave is a manifestation of wind, speech is the manifestation of thought. As the wave stirs particles of sand and algae, gesture, facial expression, and vocalization reflect the spoken word. We can appreciate the beauty of the wave with its many life-sustaining elements or we can choose to see only water crashing on the shore and spewing debris. Which do you prefer—watching a talking head or living the moment with the speaker and sharing the riches he has to offer?

Students ask, "Do I have to be mindful all the time? Isn't that exhausting? Doesn't it take too much time?" Ideally, to make mindfulness a habit, we should perform as many acts as possible carefully and with thought. Begin by noticing how often you act mindlessly— driving through a stoplight, leaving the house without your keys, taking down the wrong phone number. That kind of wasted energy is exhausting and time consuming. Mindfulness saves time because you think as you act. Slowing down and carrying out the task with mindfulness significantly reduces the chances of error and mishap.

Whenever I catch myself performing a task mindlessly, I notice that it usually takes about three times longer. For example, today I made a pitcher of grape drink from a can of concentrate. Instead of gently scooping out the contents of the can in a mindful manner, I hurriedly dumped the concentrate into the pitcher. It splashed out all over my white cabinets and sprayed specks of purple on my yellow sweater. Immediately, I had to find spot remover and a white cloth to remove the stains from my sweater. That took five minutes. Another two minutes were needed to clean off the cabinets with bleach, rinse out the rag, and wash my hands. Finishing up the grape drink required another two minutes. It took me nine minutes to complete a task that, if I had performed it in a mindful manner to start with, would have taken three minutes.

On another day, I handed my secretary a hand-written letter to type. I had composed it using a few abbreviations to save time and proofread my rough draft from my perspective only. Instead of taking thirty seconds to review the letter with my secretary or write out some of the ambiguous abbreviations, a two-paragraph letter that would have ordinarily taken five minutes to type required fifteen minutes of revisions—her time and mine.

Recently, a coworker who was about to leave for her vacation told me three vital points to include on an upcoming financial report. Feeling cocky (after all I was writing a book on listening!), I did not take that mindful twenty seconds to repeat what she had said or write it down. Two days later when writing the report, I was able to recall only about 90 percent of the information. To get that forgotten 10 percent, I had to spend another hour tracking down another source.

I'm sure you can think of a dozen examples in your own life of mindless behavior that cost you time, money, or worse. Clearly, the time spent each day cultivating mindfulness through meditation is more than compensated by increased efficiency in all your activities.

Instead of insulting yourself when mindlessness strikes, consider it a wake-up call to become mindful. Make it a point to commend yourself for the moments of mindfulness that make up your day.

Initially, it may seem like you are taking more time to carry out your tasks. You are used to doing everything in haste, so even a minute more will seem like days. Yet as your ability to concentrate improves, you will become more efficient. Tasks done mindfully are done right the first time. There is no need to recheck or redo. Mindfulness saves time.

Get Mindful

1. Choose a few activities that you normally rush through, like washing the dishes, eating your breakfast, or walking to the train. Apply mindfulness by getting all your senses involved. At first, avoid combining activities like eating and reading. Take each activity and experience every aspect for as many minutes as it takes to complete the task. While walking, feel the solidness of the earth on the soles of your shoes, notice your breathing rhythm, sense the air temperature, the breeze against your face. Offer a silent commentary as you walk: "I feel the solid earth under the soles of my feet. My breath is slow and steady. The air is cool with a hint of chimney smoke, and the wind causes the leaves to race against my feet." According to the Buddhist literature, this is called *mental noting*. By thinking or speaking aloud as you perform a task in mindfulness, your concentration stays in the present, centered on the activity. Stray thoughts of the past and future may try to intrude. Acknowledge their trespass (they may be important, like "Whoops! I forgot my umbrella!"), but get back to the present. Notice how you are completely in the present reality, totally focused on the experience of walking. Your initial experiences with mindfulness may seem like they take more time. You'll catch yourself often

thinking about other things. But as your concentration improves, you will be able to derive as much pleasure from your daily ten-minute walk as you would skiing the Rockies.

2. Do a mindfulness check periodically throughout the day. These checks can be very helpful in sharpening concentration. For instance, when I am practicing piano or playing tennis and I start to make careless mistakes, I realize that for those few seconds I imagined myself in Carnegie Hall or I was focused on winning the tennis game rather than playing my best. When I catch myself, I immediately refocus and get back to thinking about being the music or moving with the ball. In an instant, my performance improves dramatically. These slips of the mind can occur during listening too. When you notice it, refocus on your speaker. It's the same with meditation. Ideas seep into consciousness while you are trying to stay with your breath. Let them leave as gracefully as they entered. Get back to following your breath.

3. After you have made a habit staying mindful in a few simple tasks every day, apply mindfulness to listening. Begin by listening to a coworker describe a weekend or a child tell you about a baseball game. Let yourself become part of their experience from start to finish. This is very much like getting into their movie. Notice how much more of the message you absorb when you feel their delight, embarrassment, or other emotions. You'll be surprised at your ability to recall more information, including subtleties like the feeling behind the message. Notice how your thoughts do not stray and how you stay connected with your listener. Next, apply mindful listening to more factual, less engaging discussions, like your boss presenting sales objectives for the month or a lecture on quality assurance. Hear the words, but let yourself savor the motivation behind the words. Think of how these objectives or issues apply to your position and creative ways to implement them. How can you make achieving those objectives fun or more interesting?

4. We are able to listen to information at three to four times the average speaking rate. It is easy for your brain to spend that down time on other things, particularly if the information being presented is rather dry. Look for the golden nugget of opportunity by staying in the present. Instead of thinking about your shopping list or upcoming weekend activities, use that extra brainpower to review what the speaker has said thus far. Look for the possibilities associated with the topic. (We will talk more about how to pay attention in boring meetings later in the book.)

5. A simpler way to set your foundation for mindful listening is to put aside sixty seconds every day for a mindfulness minute. Plan every day, let's say at noon, to become totally immersed in the task at hand. The pleasure from that one minute spent luxuriating in the fullness of the moment, void of negativity, judgment, past, or future, will inspire more mindful minutes down the road.

Chapter Seven

Listening to Ourselves

Part 1: Our Response Is Key

There is a way between voice and presence
Where information flows
In disciplined silence it opens
With wandering talk it closes.

—Rumi

A mindful listener is one who allows the speaker to express her heart and mind and expound on her ideas without censure. If we continually cut people off or refuse to get into their movies, we ultimately discourage them from trying to connect with us.

I recall listening to several radio talk shows following the shooting deaths of twelve students and a teacher at Columbine School in Littleton, Colorado, in April 1999. Some of the talk shows consisted of high-school students discussing the possible motivations behind those who planned the assault. Inevitably, the subject of poor communication with parents or mentors emerged. Several students mentioned that they could not talk easily with their parents. Further probing by interviewers revealed that kids are put off by the *kinds of responses* they are likely to get from parents, especially if they bring up subjects like peer pressure, sex, drugs, or grades. The most dreaded responses reported by these teens were denial and advice giving. Several students said they feared negative judgment by their parents; therefore, they kept to themselves or preferred the company of peers who were less likely to pass judgment.

You can change your way of responding, not by memorizing a new list of tricks or acting differently, but by listening to yourself and becoming aware of the impact of your behavior. When you speak, notice how your words and thoughts consume your attention. The content will most likely be forgotten days or weeks after the interaction. What listeners do remember, however, is the core message of your remarks—that you were intense, full of yourself, naïve, insecure, or upbeat. This chapter introduces you to the insight of self-listening.

The first exercise for this chapter is to eavesdrop (Let's face it— we all do it!) on conversations in a restaurant or at a party, and to note the ways people respond to statements by others. Some people react by giving their point of view, adding information, or simply nodding their heads. The way you respond tells a great deal about you as a listener and the kind of person you are. Think about the people you easily open up to; think about what makes that happen. Then think about a person you find frustrating to speak with. In both cases, you will discover that their manner of responding is a major factor.

If you want to know why your kids don't talk to you, why people avoid striking up a conversation with you, start by identifying your most frequent response types.

Listed below are three statements. After reading each one, jot down on a separate sheet of paper your knee-jerk response. If you have no response, leave a blank. There are no wrong answers here.

1. A coworker says, "If my boss doesn't stop criticizing every suggestion I make, I'm going to quit and go with another group."
Your response: _____
_____
_____

2. A friend at your health club says, "I'm having a real struggle getting myself to come and work out. Between my job and the kids I have no energy for myself. Plus, I feel guilty when Janet has to stay home with the kids while I work out."
Your response:_____
_____
_____

3. Your husband says, "This is the best job offer so far! I wonder whether it's work I'll really enjoy, or do I want it for the money?"
Your response:_____
_____
_____

4. Your teenager announces, "Mr. Atkins will probably be calling you. He said I didn't write that essay—you know, the one I worked so hard on? He thinks I stole it off the Internet."

Your response:_____

_____

_____

During real interactions, notice how often your responses are more like *reactions*. When someone complains, criticizes, or states a feeling, notice how automatically statements of certain types flow from your lips. These are programmed responses, your barriers exposing themselves for the world to hear. If friends, family, and coworkers avoid connecting with you, it may be that you have allowed self-interest, prejudice, negativism, and status to take control of the conversation. On the other hand, the people you like being around forget themselves and their judgments while listening to you. Their responses reflect a selfless sensitivity to your predicament—they get into your movie!

We will now examine some response types that I call *listening stoppers*:

- **Denial**

- **Interrogation**

- **Advice giving**

- **Psychoanalysis (without a license)**

Then we'll take a look at some *listening encouragers:*

- **Silence**

- **Reassurance**

- **Paraphrasing**

Keep in mind that none of these response modes in isolation is wrong. It is just that some ways of responding are more conducive than others to enriching the conversational connection. Your challenge is to see how your comments reflect your barriers to listening. As you ease the barriers, you will notice greater flexibility in your responses; you will spontaneously be more sensitive to the perceptions of others. A forced or unnatural change in your response style is neither effective nor advised. If, however, you listen in mindfulness with a nonjudgmental ear, you will naturally respond in a way that encourages open and satisfying communication.

Denial in its pure state ("No, I didn't do it," or "No, it is not true,") has its place in the courtroom or in a confrontative situation when the facts are at stake. In these situations, something is true or it is not, and either you did it or you did not. It is important to differentiate between the constructive and destructive forms of denial. Of course we don't like it when people disagree with our point of view, but to those of us who welcome a friendly, informative debate once in awhile, denial of this sort can remove inaccuracies and educate us. To be able to outwardly disagree and support that disagreement with a sound argument is a hallmark of a competent communicator. For example, if you are negotiating an agreement and feel pressured or sense that you are being violated in some way, it is essential that you voice your objection.

It is the destructive forms of denial that affect the listening connection. For example, how often do we discount or reject another's perception of a situation? "It can't be that bad," or "You're making too much fuss about this," are perfect examples of subtle denial. Your child comes home from school after experiencing an embarrassing situation. You respond to the child's story of the event by saying, "I doubt if the kids were *really* laughing at you." Your child hears this as, "You're wrong. You are not telling me the truth. You made this up." In another situation, your child makes a derogatory statement about a classmate. By responding, "It's not nice to feel that way," or "You shouldn't say those things," you make him feel like something is wrong with him for expressing jealousy, anger, or resentment. A parent who makes a habit of denying his child's feelings is courting disaster; it is one reason kids keep things to themselves and share less and less with their parents. A mindful response could be, "That must have been very upsetting. Let's see, can we think of some ways to keep that from happening again?" This response comes naturally when you put aside your point of view and get into your child's movie.

If you encourage your teenager to share his feelings about breaking up with his girlfriend, it may be difficult to listen to him verbalize his plans for revenge. It is easy to jump in and attempt to persuade him to act like an adult, but this not only denies your teenager's hurt feelings, it denies the fact that your child is a teenager, not an adult. Your job is to listen attentively, put yourself in his movie without interrupting and judging, no matter what he proposes. When the fury dies down, you might ask, "Are there any other ways you could let her know you are upset?" or "Would you like to know what I might do in that situation?"

In the movie *Patch Adams*, actor Robin Williams demonstrated the virtues of accepting the perceptions of others versus denying them. A fellow roommate at a psychiatric hospital was unable to sleep because he had to use the bathroom. His nervous rocking in the bed kept Patch from getting any sleep. Patch asked why he didn't just walk to the bathroom. The roommate responded that he was afraid of the squirrels blocking the bathroom door. At first Patch tried to convince the roommate that he was hallucinating and that squirrels were gentle creatures, not to be feared. This only aggravated the roommate more. Then Patch got into his roommate's movie: he eliminated the squirrels in a make-believe shoot-out. Afterward, the roommate calmed down and they were both able to sleep.

Changing the subject, rolling your eyes, or ignoring your speaker's comments altogether is denial is its most pernicious form. How often do you hear Person A at the lunch table telling about her wonderful vacation visiting relatives in her home town, when Person B pipes in with, "Well, last summer we went to *Hawaii*, now *that* was a *real* vacation!" Person B has stolen the focus of the conversation and denied Person A the joy of reliving the experience and relating the exhilaration of the vacation to others. Person B has ignored the feelings of Person A. You can bet that Person A will never share any experience with Person B again.

Imagine instead that Person B chooses to get into Person A's movie by responding, "That sounds like it was very restful. Your home town, whereabouts is that?" By sharing and validating Person A's enthusiasm, Person B has created a potential ally in the workplace.

In the case of children, a lifetime of denial responses teaches them to distrust their feelings and intuition and fosters insensitivity to the feelings and needs of others.

Interrogation is one of the most exhausting responses for a speaker to hear. Have you ever come home disheartened by a discouraging event and been subjected to cross-examination by your partner with questions like, "What went wrong today?" or "Why did you do that?" or "Are you crazy?" Questions that attack, criticize, or make assumptions come across to the listener as punitive. A man misplaces his keys, and in the middle of explaining his dilemma to his wife, she interrupts in a condescending tone, "How could you do such a thing?" Such responses make the speaker feel foolish and guilty, and the result is either silence or a nasty argument.

On the other hand, open-ended questions encourage the speaker to express his feelings and may point the way to a solution. "Can you remember where you were when you last saw your keys?" or "How was your day today?" or "How do you feel about that situation?" help the speaker to relax and put his difficulties into perspective. Occasional questions by the listener that request *clarification* help to assure that the information is received accurately, such as, "So, are you saying then that frozen vegetables are more nutritious than fresh vegetables?" or "What do you mean by 'fresh' vegetables?"

However, certain types of questions can become a way of getting control of the conversation. During an informative discussion with a biological expert, a probing question like, "How does the molecular structure of a frozen vegetable differ from that of a fresh vegetable?" may be appropriate. If you are speaking to a dietician though, these deeper questions may pull the speaker away from the original intent of her message (which just may be to improve your nutrition). Asking questions as a means of manipulating the conversation usually succeeds in discouraging interaction. A mindful listener asks questions to better understand the speaker and his views. A mindless listener asks questions to fulfill her own agenda.

Beware of turning a friendly contact into an interview in which you ask endless questions but volunteer nothing about yourself. This makes it very difficult for the person being questioned to exit the conversation. He may have a difficult time figuring out whether you are truly interested in the topic or have some ulterior motive. Leave interrogating to the police and you'll have much more repeat business.

Advice giving is often linked with denial. This is frequently the mode of consultants and the eldest child in a large family. Being the eldest of five, I was often accused of this. A rule of thumb should be, *Give advice only when asked and keep it short!* When you supply unrequested advice, you may feel you are doing your listeners a great favor, but you may be totally blind to the fact that they are very capable of solving their own problems.

Sometimes what you may consider sharing information can also come across like advice giving. A good example is the new, far-from-being-a-millionaire son-in-law whose hobby is the stock market. The father-in-law makes a statement about a potential stock purchase. In the hope of winning the respect of his new and already wealthy in-laws, he remarks about his new family's stock holdings and points out flaws in their approach to staying rich. The son-in-law ignores the rather blatant lack of interest on the part of his in-laws and persists with his advice. The in-laws, clearly annoyed, try to change the subject. The son-in-law ends up feeling thwarted by the very people he wants to impress. His in-laws resent the insinuation that they cannot manage their own affairs. This young man has now set the stage for a poor relationship with his new family.

Advice, unsolicited, sends the message that the receiver is not capable of solving his own problems; it is the ultimate put-down. Remember that take-it-or-leave-it information, like giving someone a free tip or mentioning a contact that might be of interest to them, is positive. It may not always be helpful, but it is not offensive. Unrequested advice frequently takes on a preachy tone, even if it is good, sound, well-meaning advice. Chronic advice givers relish a sense of power and altruism. There's nothing more self-inflating than leaning back in your chair, slapping the desk, and starting every sentence with, "If I were you I would . . ." This response style reinforces a judgmental and status-prone barrier toward the listener.

To top it off, quite often the advice being given suits the advice-giver more than the advisee. Imagine a muscle-bound, aggressive father whose meek and frail son has just been the target of the classroom bully. After hearing about the confrontation, the father states, "Listen son, the best way to drive off a bully is to let him have it, right between the eyes!" This kind of advice is double trouble—not only did the child not request it, but the advice was insensitive to the son's disposition and physical abilities. Instead of listening to how his son felt about the altercation and the bully, the father made his son feel worse. The advice may or may not have been the right thing to do, but it was given in a mindless manner.

Advice giving can be a major obstacle to close parent-child relationships. Some kids avoid discussing problems with their parents because they give unwanted advice. (Parents, in their defense, sometimes feel that they are responsible for fixing the problem and that their advice is needed to avoid mistakes.) Over half my students report difficulties communicating with their parents. The most frequent complaint is that one or both parents are consistently judgmental and force unwanted advice on their children, disguised as so-called "guidance." Probably these parents want only to help their children, but they often forget how they saw the world in early adulthood. Parents blinded by wisdom, experience, and hard knocks may find it difficult to get into the movies of their teenagers. It takes careful self-listening and control to avoid sounding critical. Other response styles, such as paraphrasing, silence, and reassurance, are more suitable methods of building trust. Once inside your child's movie, you may notice that she has already considered many solutions for herself. Your presence as a sounding board may be all she needs.

If you can restrain yourself from responses that impose self-judgment—advice giving, interrogation, and denial—your tendency to prejudge and discriminate may lessen. Along with a reduction in negative self-talk, this will enable you to adopt a more open mind to new ideas and different perspectives.

If you are particularly prone to advice giving, you may also indulge in **psychoanalysis (without a license)**. You may feel that some deity has bestowed upon you a gift of insight so much deeper and more knowledgeable than your conversation partner's that to abstain from getting to the root of her problem is an injustice. Looking back to my high-school days, it was an introduction to existentialism that made me question life's purpose and human behavior. After several semesters of psychology classes, it was tantalizing to look for symptoms of manic depression, schizophrenia, and obsessive-compulsive disorder that could be the basis of the physical illnesses of my troubled friends and relatives.

Hours of discussion and probing self-analysis (perspectives that changed with the weather) further galvanized my tendency to make psychological diagnoses. In addition to giving advice to my younger siblings and anyone else who had the misfortune of sharing their woes with me, my new bounty of book-born wisdom led me to feel responsible for their mental health. Exasperated at their lack of follow-through on my suggestions for a happier existence, I began to examine my own behavior in a more constructive way. I saw that psychoanalyzing only prevented friends and family from sharing their feelings with me. This is also common to those who have participated successfully in counseling sessions and are eager to share their methods for overcoming fear or depression. But this kind of well-meaning help can be perceived as an invasion of privacy, and it carries the undesirable characteristics of interrogation. Like advice-giving, psychoanalysis should be left to licensed clinicians. Unless you are qualified to play Freud, it is best to remain silent and mindful.

Those of us who admit to the overuse of advice-giving and psychoanalyzing our listeners might try to get comfortable with the next response mode—**silence.** Silence is one of the most powerful response modes, but—regrettably—the least practiced. (It is important to note here the distinction between attentive silence and silence born of anger, boredom, or lack of interest. Negative silence is accompanied by fidgeting, breaking eye contact with the speaker, or otherwise withdrawing your attention. This kind of silence can be destructive to any relationship.) If you can remain silent, keeping eye contact with the person who has just spoken, you hold the key to the treasury of information to come.

Our ancestors, even as recently as our great-grandparents, were more comfortable with silence than we are today. Long ago the world had a more homogenized view of silence, where women generally deferred speaking rights to their fathers or husbands, and wise men and the elders (including women) expected lengthy silence from children as a sign of respect.

But today, most of us feel uncomfortable with silence. Our ears have accommodated a threshold of noise pollution so that a moment or two of quiet is unsettling. Perhaps this is one reason why, when someone is talking, we start thinking about what to say next, just to keep that comfort level of noise constant. We feel compelled to jump in right away and make a comment or argue the point. This nervous talk is often why we are unable to get beyond surface information to the real depth of the message. We don't allow the speaker to develop his ideas or give him the opportunity to reveal the core of his concern. As long as you continue to believe that listening is an ego-active exercise, that you need to exert control in order for the interaction to be beneficial (interrupting, questioning, advising), it will be difficult to discover the treasure of silence.

In Far Eastern cultures, silence as a behavior is revered and cherished. However, in Western cultures where fast pace and constant action reign, silence is disdained as negative and unproductive. Those who are typically silent at meetings or in group discussions tend to be viewed as indifferent and unmotivated, not team players.

When two or more of us congregate, we feel compelled to fill quiet spaces by asking too many questions, talking too much, laughing too much, or completing sentences for others. To escape silence, we look around the room, sip a drink, or clear our throats. In an elevator we try to ignore silence by staring at the numbers or the floor.

Yet in the privacy of our homes after the children have fallen asleep or under the stars on a moonlit pond, silence is our friend.

Since most of us interact daily at work or in our communities with people from different cultures, it is important to be aware of and sensitive to the varying perceptions and misinterpretations of silence to avoid intercultural misunderstandings. A cross-cultural survey taken by Satoshi Ishii and D. W. Knopf in 1976 showed that the average person in the U.S. converses twice as long (six hours and forty-three minutes) than the Japanese (three hours and thirty-one minutes). Westerners speak first, listen second, and observe third. Eastern cultures prefer a different order: observe, listen, speak.

An important feature of Japanese interpersonal relations is the notion of *enryo-sasshi*. In 1984, Ishii pointed out how the Japanese simplify their messages and avoid verbal elaboration of their ideas, depending instead upon the intuition of the listener to derive the full meaning. In his article, "Silence and Silences in Cross-Cultural Perspectives: Japan and the United States," Ishii describes "his or her psychological 'exit,' through which the encoded messages are sent out under the impact of *enryo* (reserve or restraint) is considered to be much smaller than his or her message-receiving entrance, called *sasshi*."

If you are a Westerner working abroad in an Eastern culture, it is important that you be attentive to the notion of *enryo-sasshi,* because if you talk too much and elaborate on ideas and feelings, you demonstrate poor *enryo.* This is considered rude. A person of good *sasshi,* on the other hand, is highly appreciated by others, because he is good at perceiving the whole message through the context, body language, and tone of the situation; he is viewed as wisdom seeking, open-minded.

As you begin to put mindful listening into action, your perception of silence changes. You start to notice more about the people around you. The unproductive act-like-you are-listening mode gives way to an information-gathering mindset. Your natural curiosity for learning is released from captivity after decades of stagnant, self-centered thinking. Relationships with family and coworkers become richer as silence creates space and time for understanding others.

Most of us have rarely experienced deep, true silence. We think of silence as being quiet on the outside. Deep silence, an uncomfortable bedfellow for many of us, means no internal noise either. If you've been faithful to your breathing practice, you may have experienced glimpses of true silence as the chatter in your head begins to settle down. During those rare moments, you are truly in the present, not thinking of your past mistakes nor anticipating the ones you are going to make. Uneasiness with silence of any kind is a major reason why so many of us have trouble listening. Yet, when we are given the gift of extended, attentive silence by a listener, there is a tendency to bask in its glow and reveal the depths of our soul.

One day, a statuesque, exquisitely dressed woman in her forties, whom I will refer to as Ellen, came to our voice clinic complaining about an intermittent loss of voice. Her throat exam had been normal and her voice sounded fine. She presented herself as cordial, confident, and cheerful. I began with my usual list of questions about how she used her voice every day. Ellen described herself as a high-powered executive, frequently on the phone and a presenter at meetings. For relaxation, she read voraciously, played the flute, and enjoyed a massage and facial once a week. As I imagined this lifestyle, interrupting to impose my agenda was the last thing on my mind. I was eager to determine how she was able to manage all these activities. Ellen, with her dazzling smile and somewhat boastful manner, continued to fascinate me with her enviable lifestyle as her voice became weak and breathy. She started clearing her throat, showing discomfort.

After several minutes, Ellen paused and took a deep breath. I sat stunned into silence and began to collect my thoughts in order to proceed with my assessment. Gradually, over a matter of ten seconds, a cloud came over her triumphant expression, and she began to cry softly. Now I really was in shock! I could have muttered something clinical at this point, but I didn't want to put a stop to the stream of thoughts I saw coming. In a still weaker and strained voice, Ellen spoke angrily about her troubled marriage, sick parents, and a pending lawsuit by a former coworker. More crying. Ellen finished her story with a voice very close to normal. Ellen was horribly embarrassed to have taken up my time in this manner, yet she felt tremendously relieved. She even admitted to keeping much of this information from her psychiatrist. It was clear to both of us that her episodic voice problems were stress related, and we were able to agree on an appropriate course of treatment. Looking back, it was a world's record for me to stay silent, yet it was the best thing I could have done for Ellen.

When you become absorbed with the speaker's movie, as I was (clearly my agenda took a back seat to Ellen's shocking accounts!), you don't worry about what to say next. Your speaker will appreciate your silence and relish the chance to get to the heart of the matter.

When you listen in the speaker's movie, you also tune into the silences between words—they scream with meaning. Disappointment, reluctance, heartbreak, anticipation, remorse, hopefulness, and anything else the speaker cannot effectively put into words become loud and clear in the silences. Many of the emotional casualties in our lives stem from attending only to the words, the footprints and shadows of the message, and we regard that as "listening."

Too often those moments needed to elaborate on a feeling are cut off by questions, comments, or a change of subject. I recall doing these same things because I felt uncomfortable with silence. It was important for me to take control of the session and get on with my agenda to treat the patient. It took Ellen to teach me that attentive, supportive silence is often the best treatment. For Ellen, it was the catalyst for her to see the connection between her anxiety and her voice.

There are similar situations with patients referred to me for presurgical counseling. They may have cancer of the larynx and must have the voice box removed. You cannot imagine how devastating this can be, particularly to anyone who uses his voice for a living. My job is to inform them of the alternatives for communicating after surgery. Occasionally I get a patient, angry about the upcoming surgery, whose voice complaints were ignored or misdiagnosed. They may have acquired reputations for being problem patients. These patients need to express their feelings, but are discouraged by hearing responses like denial and advice giving. The last thing they want to hear about is an artificial voice substitute. In these situations, I introduce myself and let them know that I will be able to help them communicate after surgery. Then I ask them how they are doing. From then on, I remain silent and get into their movie. Immediately, they recount their experience, tell about their families, or their deepest concerns. They may cry and even scream out their anguish. Sometimes they need to be reassured about the surgeon's credentials or their fear of dying in surgery. They cannot discuss many of these issues with their spouses. By the end of the meeting, they often apologize for their outbursts, and in the same breath, thank me profusely for helping them. Despite the fact that I never get to my agenda, they still feel I do them a great service.

Silence is virtuous in its ability to make your speaker feel good about himself. Silence allows the speaker's deeper thoughts to surface, thoughts that often contain solutions to problems. When you allow your speaker the time to think out loud in a supportive environment, you set the stage for her empowerment, and she will want to be in your company more often.

Silence is also a powerful negotiation tool. Your speaker's real priorities may not be the parcel of land or the salary. Perhaps what he really fears is loss of prestige or control. If a worker demands a raise and shorter hours, he may be complaining about the cost and flexibility of the daycare center at your facility. By making room for silence, the real issues come to the surface, thus short-circuiting hours of unproductive arguing and escalating antagonism.

On the lighter side, I must make a confession. I often find silence quite entertaining. In the past it was more common for me to share my experiences equally with my speaker, but more often these days I find it enjoyable to hold myself back from sharing my experiences, particularly when the speaker is having one heck of a time telling hers.

For example, one day my husband and I were walking in the woods with our dog. We came across another beautiful dog, Chester, and his owner, Kate. Kate is a fascinating woman whom I run into every so often. She always has some unusual insight to share. This time she started talking about the spiritual nature of dogs and their connection to man. Being a dog lover myself, I could relate to her point of view. At first I felt a bit of an urge to jump in and share my feelings and experiences, but drew myself back into her movie because she was so exuberant in support of her theory. My contribution would have added little, and I didn't feel a personal need for feedback. It was just plain interesting to listen to her. Kate went on to talk about yoga and how it had changed her life. I too practice yoga regularly and find it extremely helpful. I would have liked to let her know that I share her interest, but she left no room for interruption. And the best part was that it was okay! I did not feel the least bit slighted nor did I need to focus the conversation on myself—I was totally in Kate's movie. As we neared the gate, Kate mentioned how she hoped someday to write a book about dogs and asked me what I knew about book writing. I mentioned that, as a matter of fact, I was in the process of writing a book. She asked me the topic. I told her it was about listening. Needless to say, Kate was embarrassed by having done so little listening throughout our walk. To reassure her, I told her how interesting her insights were and how I thoroughly enjoyed hearing her point of view. Kate commented, "Even though I did all the talking, it felt so good to have someone feel the same way I do!" I realized that silence is a form of sharing.

Notice too, when you are in your speaker's movie, how relaxed and tuned in your posture becomes. Chances are, you are keeping eye contact with the speaker, occasionally nodding your head, and leaning slightly forward. Silence is not so uncomfortable when you are in the speaker's movie, because you naturally listen with your whole body—just like at the theater! Your posture and facial expression naturally react to the message and the messenger. There is no space for self-conscious noise or thinking about past or future. Your mind is centered on receiving not only the speaker's words and gestures, but the feeling behind the message. (Later, I will discuss how silence can be a powerful ally when listening under stress.)

Comforting a friend suffering through difficult times is never easy. You feel you have to say something in order to show that you share their feelings. In these situations supportive silence is the best response. By offering silent support, you encourage your speakers to describe their feelings, vent anger and frustration, and relate their problems in detail. You *are* responding by simply not talking.

Closely linked to silence is appropriate and supportive **reassurance**. Statements like, "Yes, I see that your situation must be very difficult," or "I'm sure you'll do the right thing," restore confidence and courage. These kinds of responses are devoid of judgment and denial of their pain; they reassure your friend that you empathize with him. Although it can be comforting to know that other people have experienced the same feelings and survived, most persons in the immediate stress of job loss or family tragedy cannot derive comfort from hearing you relate a similar experience or pointing out the silver lining to their black cloud.

When reassurance is sincere, accompanied by a warm voice and a simple gesture, it is appreciated. For example, Bob comes home after a difficult day at the office. He laments to his wife, Kelly, that he is burned-out tired of the politics at work and feels no challenge. Both parties know there is no immediate solution to the problem— money is tight and the jobs in his field are not plentiful. If Kelly were to suggest he just quit, this would cause an argument. What Bob needs right now is reassurance and support. A comment like, "I know you try every day to make the best of this situation; I really admire your patience," is just the right touch. However, a reassuring response that lacks sincerity may come across as condescending or insensitive to the speaker's experience.

A medical student once told me about an attending physician who forbade students to tell their patients, "I understand." The physician warned that unless they had personally experienced the patient's disease and its emotional side effects, it was dishonest to claim understanding of the patient's predicament.

Many attempts to reassure someone after loss of a loved one often backfire. Old standby comments like, "At least she isn't suffering," and "You know he's in a better place," are subtle ways to avoid a bereaved person's movie. We don't want to be dragged down into their sorrow, so we say such things to distance the distressed person from his emotions and get back in control. What those beset by tragedy need is to talk about their loved ones. Attentive silence and empathy, not sympathy, are most appreciated.

Paraphrasing is one of my favorite response styles because it provides much for both speaker and listener. Paraphrasing is the act of repeating back your speaker's message for the purpose of clarity and reflection. It is a way to let her know you're doing your best to understand. It also serves as a way of hearing the message again to more deeply process the meaning behind the words.

Mindful listeners are sensitive to two variations of paraphrasing: *parroting* (repeating back as exactly as possible what the speaker says), and *summarizing* (putting into our own words the gist of our speaker's message). Parroting should be used when exact information like numbers, times and dates, or other precise details are concerned. For example, I say to my secretary, "Lori, please make three copies of that report. Send the original to Mr. Smith, and one copy each to Dr. Jones and Dr. Jackson. The third ones goes into my file." Lori parrots my request by saying, "So you want me to send the original to Mr. Smith, a copy to Dr. Jones, a copy to Dr. Jackson, and put the third copy in your file." By this response, I know with certainty that I have communicated the information correctly. I get a chance to hear back what I said and make any clarification that's needed, and I feel confident that the task will be carried out correctly. By parroting back the message, Lori had a chance to hear it again too. She feels confident that she can do what needs to be done.

This style of responding is most helpful when taking directions. How often have you stopped a stranger for directions and could not remember what he told you? Your negative self-talk distracted you from being in the moment. You thank him, roll up the window and try to find someone else.

Let's redo this scenario in mindfulness, using paraphrasing as a way to clarify the directions and store them in memory. You stop and ask the stranger for directions and visualize the route as he describes it. In your mind's eye, you see the left at the light, and the right at the stop sign. After he's finished, say, "Let me be sure I have this straight," and you proceed to repeat the directions. So far, I have never yet found a stranger who objected to this. Paraphrasing is a practical and time-saving approach to effective communication. When you correctly state back the information in your own words, both parties are satisfied that the message was received.

Summarizing to assure that the speaker's needs and/or feelings have been understood is usually the first step in firming up a relationship. This checking in to see if you're on the same page can be helpful in a stressful interaction or in a negotiation, because in heated discussions we are not good at hearing or saying the right words; then we get angry when the other person interprets us wrongly. As a mindful listener, you get deep in the speaker's movie, synthesize the words, gestures, facial expressions, and tone of voice to arrive at the best guess, but it is still only a guess. That is why you need to check with the speaker. It may mean asking a question like, "Are you saying that you'd rather I have more normal working hours?" Or it may be in a statement, like "I sense you're discouraged with this project and you'd like to switch to a different one." Sometimes it takes a mindful listener to sum things up for a speaker, to clarify the thoughts or the vibes they are sending out.

Irene, your employee, comes into your office one day and gives notice. She explains that a highway construction project near her home makes the morning commute impossible to predict, and moreover, she has a teenager with some serious behavioral problems. The result is that Irene is frequently late for work, and although she makes sure her phone is answered until she arrives, she feels guilty asking others to cover for her.

In this case, it would be clearly unproductive for you to parrot back all the grisly details. Instead, summarizing her explanation lets her know she's been heard. "Irene, I understand that things are quite hectic for you at home right now. You really enjoy working here, and I see that you've tried to make other arrangements, but you feel obligated to offer your resignation because you have to rely on others for coverage. Do I understand you correctly?" Irene nods her head, and the expression of relief on her face is unmistakable. Your summary of her problem opens the path toward a solution other than quitting her job, such as shorter hours or a different starting time.

When I summarize in this way, my conversation partners are often relieved—as Irene was—to hear the words that they *wanted* to say. Other times, my attempts to clarify the message are off the mark and I need to be set straight. In either case, paraphrasing by summarizing pays off. In contrast, parroting in situations where feelings and volatile emotions are involved can come across as sarcastic or condescending. Summarizing, on the other hand, sends the subliminal message, "I am repeating what I think you said, because I really want to understand your viewpoint."

Paraphrasing is also a way—without being judgmental or hinting at advice—of getting people to reflect on what they communicate. Suicide-prevention hotlines teach their counselors to paraphrase as a way of clarifying a caller's view on a problem and getting him to continue talking. Since there is no visual communication, it is important to let the troubled caller know with more than a few "Uh-huhs" that the counselor is listening.

In my classes, the paraphrasing exercise can be painfully surprising. It exposes weaknesses in attention and memory, yet with practice it quickly improves focus and retention. One student reads a two- or three-step direction or a short, informative paragraph to a partner. The partner has to paraphrase. The reader then provides feedback on accuracy and, if necessary, clarifies the information. After the first several minutes of this exercise, it is easy to see why we often lose information and make so many listening mistakes.

Paraphrasing has been criticized as an unnatural way of responding. To these criticisms I say, yes, paraphrasing, like any other response style, can be overused and become mechanical. And, yes, it sounds strange to let your speaker know you want to be sure you got his message—but isn't that what good communication is all about? If you understand the purpose of paraphrasing, you will tend to be conservative in its use.

I make paraphrasing a regular component of voice therapy. At our first visit, I encourage my higher-functioning patients to ask questions if there is something they don't understand, because I'll be checking periodically to make sure they do. This immediately sets the stage for more active participation on their part. After explaining the goal of the session and going through a series of exercises to meet that goal, I often ask the patient, "Why did we do those exercises? What was the point?" If the patient cannot answer correctly, i.e., is not able to paraphrase the goal of the session, then I know the patient was not listening, did not understand, or I did not explain it clearly. In the latter case, the patient may not have given me any verbal or nonverbal indication that she did not understand.

With practice, the patient becomes more involved with the session because she knows that she has to make the link between what she is trying to achieve and how she is going to do it. After telling back her understanding of the session, she is more motivated to practice the exercises, since she understands the connection with the goal. I know this because she was able to verbalize it. I also apply these same techniques with my students. A student describes an exercise and carries it out correctly. At the end of the session, it might go like this:

Me: Today you came with questions about coordinating your breath support and vocal pitch. Now that we've reviewed that process, is it clearer?

Patient: Yes. I can do both now and it sounds and feels better.

Me: I need to be sure that I have explained these ideas clearly. Please tell me how you understand this method and then demonstrate the process.

After the student explains and demonstrates the exercise, I clarify any weaknesses. The student and I are both satisfied with the session. The student has achieved another skill level, and we have both made an investment in the learning process.

This form of paraphrasing is appropriate in any teacher-student situation because both share the same interest—to correctly execute the process to achieve a positive outcome. Many people are reluctant to ask questions. They don't want to appear stupid, they don't want to take up your time, and/or in the past they have not had patient instructors. In any teaching or sales interaction, encourage your speakers to tell back how they understand the procedure so you can be sure that you communicated the information correctly. Let them know that mistakes are fine. Do not judge their responses as right or wrong; just offer *clarification*. It is important to you, for instance, that they understand how to use the equipment you are selling them. Chances are, they will be grateful and remember the time you took to listen to their questions in order to make them happy customers.

Honest communication between customer and salesperson, teacher and student, or therapist and patient is essential to success; both parties must see themselves as equal partners. In a balanced, barrierless environment, students and patients feel comfortable enough to ask questions, clarify problems with the learning process, and openly discuss their progress. Paraphrasing invites this give and take. Make paraphrasing a habit in these situations, and note how your confidence in your ability to process information soars!

To be agile in the use of these and other ways of responding requires self-listening and practice. Remember that response styles are situation dependent. If, however, you let yourself into the speaker's movie and forget your own agenda for awhile, you will become more sensitive to their needs and hear yourself respond in a more varied and sensitive manner. Keep in mind the many different combinations of responses you may give. In the above examples, silence and reassurance are comfortable partners. Paraphrasing combines well with any of the response types when clarification is required.

Examining your habitual responses to your speakers helps you better understand your attitude toward listening to others. When you converse with others, you and your listeners find out who you really are. For example, advice giving, denial, and interrogation are *self-centered* response styles, and they send the message of aggressive, ego-driven closed mindedness. Conversely, paraphrasing, silence, and

reassurance are *speaker-supportive* styles. If you develop these qualities, your speakers will perceive you as secure with yourself, open to
new ideas, and caring.

Now, go back to the first exercise at the beginning of this chapter and label your responses. What kind of message about yourself
did you plant? During your next conversation or while listening to
others, notice how the majority of preferred listeners (those that we
feel a connection with) predominantly support the speaker, while
poor listeners support themselves.

Catch Yourself

1. As you read through this chapter, you were probably able to identify with a few habitual response modes.
Notice how often you use these modes during an average
day, and make note of the reactions you get. Think how
you might have responded differently, using some of the
other response types.

2. Sit back and listen to conversations. See if you can
identify some of the more common response types. Notice the reaction of speakers to certain responses. Think of
how you might have responded. Note too the combination of responses a good listener offers.

3. Here are seven statements that might be directed
to you from different people. Using what you have learned
about mindful responding, what would you say or *not* say
in response to these statements:

- I'm leaving my wife.

- I have the hardest time meeting nice men.

- Do you think I need to see a counselor?

- The government should ship these good-for-nothing immigrants back home.

- My wife tells me I need Viagra.

- I just can't get into an exercise habit.

- I look fat and frumpy in this suit.

4. Pick one of the more powerful modes (such as silence or paraphrasing) and apply it at least once a day. Select a person with whom you frequently converse. Let her talk. Avoid interrupting. Don't take the stage from her. Don't try to teach her anything. Be silent, or if she looks like she wants feedback, paraphrase what she told you without making a judgment. Notice how much more she wants to share with you and how much more you learn about her.

5. Get more practice with paraphrasing. There are several ways to make this a habit. The next time you're out walking, stop someone and ask for directions to a nearby destination. Repeat the directions for confirmation. Both you and the person you stopped will feel good that the directions were communicated correctly. Another way is to paraphrase with someone who accuses you of *not* listening. Show that you are making an effort by repeating

in your own words what he said. Notice how after only a few times, he will likely make a comment that you are paying more attention. In some relationships, this little bit of effort on your part can mean the world to your partner.

6. Encourage others to paraphrase you. If your child has trouble following directions in school, ask him to re-peat simple instructions like, "David, please go upstairs and get the blue sweater from your drawer and give it to Mike. Now, tell me back what I just said." Reward him for his cooperation and notice how every time he succeeds, his self-esteem zooms.

7. If you are faithful to your daily breathing practice, you will naturally become more comfortable with silence. As you center your concentration on the breath, notice how your mind noise settles down. Your tendency to start thinking about what you're going to say while the other person is still talking will be reduced. The more you prac-tice, the longer you will be able to sustain a mindful listener's composure, free from barriers and internal dis-traction. Your responses will reflect your speaker's needs and less self-interest.

Chapter Eight

Listening to Ourselves

Part 2: The Listener's Pariahs

Blessed is the man who, having nothing to say,
abstains from giving us worthy evidence of the fact.
—George Eliot

*I*f we could listen to ourselves as we converse, we would probably be astounded at how often we speak mindlessly. We are so taken up with being the speaker that, quite innocently perhaps, we make insensitive comments, speak inaccurately, or talk too much, hardly aware of the effect of those actions. Mindless speaking is a proven listening stopper.

For example, I was recently corrected by a patient, notorious for her attention to detail, for using the word *girl* to refer to a twenty-year-old woman who worked at the desk. I meant no harm by that slip of the tongue, but in the eyes of my patient it was offensive.

Having heard that I was from Chicago, a native New Englander asked me if I noticed any differences between Bostonians and Chicagoans. In the past I might have mindlessly responded that I felt that people in Boston tend to be less friendly and more conservative. These words would have certainly ruffled his feathers. Now when I'm asked such a question, I try to consider my listener *before* I speak. I might say, "Bostonians appear to me to be more private," or "Bostonians take a little more time to get to know strangers." Both statements communicate my perceptions without hurting anyone's feelings.

The last time you were faced with an angry customer, did you make things worse by giving excuses or stating company policy? *Ugh!* According to Jeffrey Gitomer, public relations consultant, customers hate the word *policy.* The next time, shift your perspective to the customer's concerns. You might say, "Yes, that's terrible. The fastest way to handle that is . . ." It is likely that you will keep that customer.

Think of the times when others have offended you. Did they say those things on purpose? Couldn't they sense your embarrassment or irritation despite your smile? No, probably not. They were deep in their own movies, unaware of yours.

Mindless speaking is so annoying that perhaps it is one of the reasons we dwell more and more in removed forms of communication like e-mail, Internet chat rooms, and faxes. We make the connections we crave but avoid the hassles associated with face-to-face contact. Occasionally, I get students who sign up for my listening course at the behest of their employers. These students admit that they prefer to distance themselves from customers at all costs. They often complain about the inefficiency and dissatisfaction they experience in face-to-face or telephone contact, not just with customers, but sometimes even family and friends. Some avoid personal contact because people don't get to the point, they act foolishly, laugh too much, and beat around the bush. They interrupt, complain, judge, give unrequested advice, and talk too much. To them and a growing number of onliners, most people are to be avoided.

Denial, endless interrogation, or the dreaded advice-giving responses are just a few of the gaffs that can be avoided with a bit of mindfulness. Try being your own customer for a change. Call into your office with a question or a complaint, preferably late in the day (about ten minutes before closing time is good). How well are you treated? When you hang up the phone, how do you feel? Great or offended? Respected or resentful? Listen to your voice mail. What's your perception? Do you feel welcomed or like a number? Is there even a hint of sincerity in that voice about your call being important?

Interestingly, the more mindful you are of the movies of your speakers, the more sensitive you become to your own words. The next time you say something you regret, notice whether you were propelled by self-consciousness, ego fulfillment, or disrespect for the speaker's perspective. Smile at your newfound awareness, knowing that this discovery will prevent future mindless moments. Avoid putting yourself down. Instead, remember that your intentions were good. Next time, notice how much more appropriate your comments are when you are mindful of not only your intent, but the perspective of your listener. You will say less and learn more. Your mind won't wander around looking for a clever rejoinder so that your conversation partner can see how witty and amusing you are.

One of the benefits of meditation is that you learn to pause before you speak. Meditation deautomatizes your false self, the part of the ego that is self-conscious, insecure, righteous, and deluded by your barriers. If your foundation for listening is not based on meditation and mindfulness, it feels awkward and mechanical to stop and think before speaking. You have to first clear your mind of traffic, stop wondering what the other person is thinking about you, get comfortable with the silence, try to remember what the speaker just said, and formulate a response. Drudgery of this sort discourages you from making self-listening a habit. Fortunately, daily mindfulness practice makes it comfortable and natural to take in the whole message and choose your words carefully in much less time and with greater accuracy. Your words must match as closely as possible how you feel and what you want. However, there are many interpretations out there. Aside from words alone, other features of your speech can flip the meaning. Varying combinations of characteristics like speech rate, pauses, pitch contour, emphasis, loudness, facial expression, and eye contact may concoct a message well beyond your intent.

Mindful listening includes the ability to listen to what you say and make necessary changes. When writing a memo, you are more careful with word choice. Because you can *see* what you want to communicate, it is easier to review your message and edit vague or inaccurate information. Why should you be any less careful when speaking? How many times have you said "left" when you meant "right," or "Tuesday morning" when you meant to say, "Thursday morning" and later paid the consequences?

Just as you carefully watch your footing on a steep and rocky path, you should speak with the same care to avoid injury or costly mistakes. You make a statement, hear it back in your head, and study your listener to be sure it was received the way you meant it. If you notice frequent discrepancies between your intention and the reaction of your listener, you need to examine whether 1) your words accurately represented your thoughts, 2) your tone of voice or physical movements contradicted your intended meaning, 3) your listener interpreted your meaning from his unique cultural perspective rather than yours, or 4) your listener chose not to accept your point of view or did not process the information accurately. Listening to yourself, like listening to others, is an art. It requires mindfulness to match your intent with appropriate words and be sensitive to the way others perceive them.

Earlier, I described how barriers are serious impediments to your ability to listen to others. They also get in the way of listening to yourself. In the examples that follow, notice how status, personal agenda, and negative self-talk can sabotage the intent of your message. A mindful listener needs to eliminate these barriers when listening to herself and others.

Entering the movies of your listeners is as close as you can get to understanding them. You cannot read people's minds and walk on eggshells all the time, but you can prevent hurt feelings and careless errors by being more sensitive in delicate situations. The ability to listen to yourself while keeping your speaker in mind may include giving directions, personal heart-to-heart discussions, and interviews. Take a moment to think about situations when a bit more self-listening would have resulted in a better outcome. Let's take a look at some of our less desirable speaking habits.

Swearing, to spark a listener's attention or to show displeasure, should be avoided. More often than not, swear words or obscenities are a turn-off and suggest an inability to express yourself in a more intelligent manner. Even expressions like "gosh," or "darn it" have been known to ruffle feathers in certain company. Especially in formal settings, you should refrain from expressions that can be considered disrespectful or inappropriate, like "Jesus, Mary, and Joseph!" or "Gosh darn it!" These expressions may not only affect your credibility, they may also offend.

Are you a chronic interrupter? **Interrupting,** or cutting off the speaker and taking over the conversation, is *the* number-one most annoying conversation habit. It is a discourteous and egocentric way of conversation control. When you consistently interrupt, it is likely that your preoccupation with status or self is rearing its ugly head. You may also interrupt by finishing a sentence for the speaker. In doing so, you assure the speaker (and everyone else in the conversation circle) that you have saved everyone time by reading the speaker's mind and anticipating what he is going to say. How chagrined you are when you guess wrong!

These days, the length of the average doctor's appointment is between ten and fifteen minutes. Physicians are pressed to make the most of a very short period of time. Sometimes, out of necessity to complete the examination in a timely manner, interruption may be necessary, yet this is not always the case. Observational studies show that the average duration of a physician listening without interrupting a patient is seventeen seconds. If patients are allowed to speak until they finish, they stop talking in about forty-five seconds. Patient satisfaction measures show that if the physician interrupts, both parties are dissatisfied. If the physician listens without interrupting, both parties give higher evaluations of the visit.

It is easy for a consultant in any field to see the value of relinquishing control of the interaction for the first forty-five seconds or so. Think about it! *Less than a minute* can make all the difference between open, honest communication and feeling rushed and treated impersonally.

Yet not all interrupting is bad. At times you can break into someone's explanation in a positive way with an encouraging comment like, "Oh, yeah, I wanted to hear about this," or an emphasis that adds humor, such as, "Right, *very* big shoes!" These positive forms of interruption are inoffensive and demonstrate interest and coparticipation in topic development. If you listen hard to a group conversation, you will hear a wide variety of rude interruptions and some congenial interrupting-like behaviors. But where do you draw the line? When does merely interjecting become interrupting?

Deborah Tannen in her book, *Talking from 9 to 5,* uses the term *overlapping* to neutralize the negative connotation associated with interruption. Linguists Carl Zimmerman and Candace West (1975) describe overlapping as instances of simultaneous speech where a speaker other than the current speaker begins to speak at or very close to a possible transition place in a current speaker's utterance (i.e., within the boundaries of the last word). Tannen claims that an overlap becomes an interruption when the *balance* of the conversation is disrupted. If one speaker repeatedly jumps in on the original speaker with comments or attempts to change the topic and causes the original speaker to give way, the resulting communication is unbalanced. There is symmetry, however, when both parties equally take turns, that is, build on an idea or argue a point in which there is no winner or loser. Tannen says that a symmetrical struggle for the floor can be described as creating rapport in the spirit of ritual opposition analogous to sports.

Basic to whether an individual is overlapping or interrupting is the intent of such remarks. The quality of intent may be communicated by the timing of the interjection, the words used, and the show of emotion behind the words. If your aim is to support and establish rapport with your speaker, then your interjections will be considered positive. If, however, your intent is to take the floor and dominate your conversation partner, then a negative form of interruption is perceived. You need to be sensitive to the fact that many of your conversation partners may not appreciate even the positive forms of interruption. (On the other hand, in a debate, negative forms of interruption may be hailed as signs of leadership—and therefore positive.) Tannen states that in judging whether an overlap is an interruption, context is important (casual conversation versus a job interview), as well as a speaker's personal style (high- versus low-involvement types), and how different styles interact.

You may also interrupt the speaker in nonverbal ways. Frequent shifts in your posture or looking away are distracting to a speaker and can be interpreted as wanting to *break into* the speaker's monologue or *break away* from the speaker. When you are in the speaker's movie, your body language naturally conforms to the message. Your position rarely changes, your eye contact is fairly constant. You may interject a gesture or vocalization like a nod or an "Uh-huh," signaling "Yes, I'm listening." An overlapping or interruptive gesture may be a raised finger, a touch on the arm, or leaning forward toward the speaker. To allow for taking turns in a discussion encourages cooperative listening. A good listener encourages the speaker to continue developing her idea through a combination of silence, good eye contact, and verbal support. A good listener avoids any selfish attempt to interrupt the speaker's stream of consciousness.

Talking too much is quite often the result of the fear of silence. When a person is labeled as talking too much, it usually means that he talks on and on about things that interest only himself.

I am convinced that a speaker who goes on and on for days, totally oblivious to the glazed look in your eyes, utterly consumed by the sound of her voice, feels that she is doing *you* an immense favor. How many times have you been subjected to an extreme version of mindless speaking at a party or work gathering? To refresh your memory and make you take a closer look at your own behavior, let's relive a minute with a listener's pariah.

A friendly individual walks up to you, eager to talk, and starts speaking enthusiastically about some gossip at the office. You realize that, due to the inappropriateness of the subject material, this is *not* the movie you want to be in. The speaker does not pick up on your queasy facial expression, but instead insists on dragging you down into the abyss. You are stuck and at a loss as to how you can gracefully remove yourself from this one-sided conversation.

Or how about a situation in which the speaker takes *forever* to get to the point? Not only do you have to endure the introduction, but the worst is yet to come! These people are so into their movies that they are blind to the sweat dripping from your brow. They don't notice you fidgeting in your seat, shifting your weight, or looking around the room for rescue! They just keep talking, frequently looking off somewhere else. When this happens I get the urge to slip away to see if that person even notices I'm gone. I feel I'm being used as a prop for the speaker. Then, to make matters worse, they start dropping names or using buzz words they know you are not familiar with. By this time, you are praying for a miracle! Abduction by alien beings, a call from the IRS, even a small earthquake will do—*anything* but having to listen to this rambling! While the nausea still lingers in reliving this all too familiar scene, let's make a sincere commitment to avoid being a listener's pariah. Just because an experience was funny, exciting, or interesting to you, doesn't mean it will be to anyone else.

Mindful self-listening means answering questions directly, choosing topics that are appropriate to the conversation, and selecting your words carefully so that they reflect your true meaning. Avoid telling stories and opening up topics that are of interest only to you. Having to sit through a story that doesn't go anywhere or the relentless pursuit of a topic that bores or offends you is a particularly refined form of social torture. Some of these people won't quit unless you see things their way (you have to admit the virtues of red meat even though you are a staunch vegetarian, or vice-versa).

I once had a client who was a marketing consultant. His most valuable piece of advice was, "Stop talking after the customer says yes." After winning a sale, your excitement may open the door to mindless talking—making promises you can't keep, excessive thanking, putting down the competition. Your customer may wonder whether he made the right choice.

Quite often I am asked, "How do you deal with someone who just doesn't stop talking? What about the person who rambles on and on?" If you find yourself in an interview with a prospective employee, a customer, or someone at a cocktail party who talks mindlessly, there are graceful ways to cut to the chase without offending the speaker. One way to get the speaker back on track is to say, "Excuse me, John, perhaps I was not clear enough in my question. I asked if . . ." Often, the speaker has forgotten the question and just keeps talking in the hope of remembering. We hear this frequently on radio talk shows. The interviewer asks a two- or three-part question and the guest goes off on a tangent that answers only a part of the original question.

In healthcare it is not at all uncommon to have several patients a day who have a lot to tell; perhaps a visit to the hospital is the only social life they have. And as we will discuss later, being heard is the first step to healing. However, the reality is that healthcare and other kinds of workers who deal with the public have a limited amount of time to spend with each customer. I deal with this predicament by imagining the time I can spend listening each day as an armful of cookies. (As I get to be a more mindful person, I hope that I can add a few more cookies to my load). Unfortunately, I can carry only a finite number of cookies each day.

Some people may need more cookies than others, but the fact remains, I have just so many. After listening mindfully for as many minutes as I can spare, I may have to interrupt and say, "Excuse me, Mr. Johnson, I wish I had more time to listen, but I have to see the next person on my list. Would you write down anything else you'd like to tell me and leave that note in my box? I'll get back to you by tomorrow." Only occasionally do people feel that they need to leave the note. Sometimes, writing down their comments or questions helps them crystallize their thoughts or realize that those questions were already addressed. Being as honest as possible about why you need to stop listening leaves the customer satisfied and allows him to put closure on the meeting.

Many times I am asked, "If someone starts talking about something I'm not interested in, should I be polite and keep acting like I'm listening or interrupt the speaker?" Most people agree that they would rather be interrupted than have someone pretend that they are listening. And the longer you wait to exit the conversation, the more uncomfortable exiting becomes. In the rare case when I feel I do not have the patience, interest, or time to listen, I simply excuse myself early on in a polite tone and tell the speaker that I need to move along. I refuse to make up bogus excuses. It's bad enough when people don't want to hear what you have to say; to get a phony excuse for exiting is often more hurtful. Instead, I simply stay true to myself and my notion that I have just so many cookies to share in one day. Keep in mind, though, that there are times when people really need a few extra cookies (that includes ourselves!). That is when patience is most appreciated. Sometimes, the nicest thing you can do for someone is listen.

I had an opportunity to sit in on a meeting of a newly appointed vice president and his ten department managers. After reviewing the corporation's annual goals, the VP requested that each manager present a brief summary of his department's current projects and challenges. He asked, "In your description, keep in mind how you might relate to each other's circumstances so that we can team up on some of these projects." The VP added that the meeting needed to adjourn in thirty minutes, clearly, a polite request to keep it short. Only *four of the ten managers* appeared to be mindful of their responsibility. These four presented their projects in terms understandable to the other managers. Their descriptions were concise and details were kept to a minimum. These managers remembered the VP's request to link their concerns with the interests of the other team members. They made eye contact with everyone in the group and kept to their three-minute allotment. The VP, a mindful communicator himself, gleefully praised these managers' ability to focus and show respect to the other members of the group.

The meeting went eighteen minutes overtime, thanks to one manager who talked nonstop for almost ten minutes. To this day, when asked to give a brief update, he is often teased by his coworkers as one who needs a stopwatch. A reputation as a poor self-listener is often hard to shake. It was evident from the pressed half-smile on the face of the VP that he knew exactly whom he could count on to meet deadlines, think on their feet, and work as team players.

Does it seem like barriers were at work here? We see from this meeting that not only can those great walls separate you from the speaker (as discussed in chapter four), but they can isolate you from your listeners as well; your vice president is probably not the person from whom you want to estrange yourself. Ironically, most of these six managers were known to be very hard workers, staying late and often working weekends. In fact, at least four of the six showed such intense involvement with their agendas that they appeared totally unaware of their unteamlike approach and hard-to-listen-to presentations. Could they be any better listeners with their staffs? Not likely.

Other mindless self-listening behaviors that we often encounter in long-winded meetings include:

- using unfamiliar jargon and acronyms, such as "the MAC project"
- giving too many details
- inserting anecdotes
- incessant use of "um" or "uh"
- dropping names
- long pauses
- avoiding eye contact with the audience
- interrupting a speaker to ask tangential questions
- making self-deprecating comments

The last is frequently a vice of new managers; for example, "Well, I'm not very good at speaking by the clock," or "I hope I remember everything that's going on in my department." The care you take to choose your words and consider your audience tells much about your competency and your ability to respect others. If you are accused of talking too much, it may imply that you do not allow others to take a turn. Quite often we are so engrossed in our own movies that we neglect obvious signals that it is time to give someone else a chance to speak. A good rule of thumb is to keep your comments to twenty seconds or less. When you go beyond this limit, you push the listener's attention span. Be sensitive to nonverbal cues by others who may want their turn to speak. Such a person may

- shift her position in the chair,

- signal for a turn by raising his index finger,

- lean forward and audibly inhale,

- break eye contact with you,

- nod quickly and open his mouth as if to begin speaking.

Observe the difference between interruptive behaviors discussed earlier and preinterruptive gestures intended as turn-taking requests. Acknowledging these is part of being a mindful and considerate listener.

How often do you begin sentences with *I*? The syntax of the English language promotes the use of the first-person pronoun at the beginning of sentences to signal the arrival of your opinion or experience of the self. The use of *I* in a prominent position in a sentence reflects our culture's emphasis on self-interest. Your agenda (mentioned in chapter four), better known as the me-myself-and-I barrier, is the greatest obstacle to listening to others *and* ourselves.

The repetitive use of *I* has the tendency to alienate your listener. For example, at a recent medical conference, a woman in the audience frequently chimed in to relate her experience with whatever new methods of treatment the trainer introduced. She started most of her statements with *I,* or *I* was used prominently in the sentence: "*I* liked that approach because *I* felt it applied to the kind of patients *I* work with," or "*I* don't agree with that according to what *I* have researched." After a half day of this, groans from the audience signaled that she had alienated others in the group. Her lengthy comments were interpreted as arrogant and self-serving.

Recently, I attended a group swimming class taught by two well-known triathletes. Each student swam his heart out hoping for a helpful critique of his stroke. Each coach started with five students. Both coaches were equally friendly and experienced, but there was one crucial difference: one of the coaches *consistently* referred to himself when asked a question. For example, a beginner asked, "How can I improve my swimming speed?" The coach answered, "Well, when *I* started out *I* began using a stop watch and improved my time by a few seconds each lap." Subsequent answers included, "Well, *I* use . . ." and "What *I* do . . ." These responses were discouraging. What the students wanted were answers that took *their* unique situations, such as physical condition, years swimming, and level of ability into consideration. The use of the me-myself-and-I barrier was a listening stopper. The other coach gave pretty much the same advice, but couched it in different language, such as, "You might try timing your laps—that is, if you can already swim a half mile with some ease," or asking questions about what the student had already tried. Overuse of *I* tends to alienate listeners and decrease trust. Keeping your ego out of the spotlight when giving requested advice creates admiration and a willingness to follow through, because the needs of your speakers are taken into consideration.

This offensive use of *I* was pointed out to a friend of mine who lived with two other people who received few phone calls. Because 90 percent of the calls were for my friend, she innocently recorded her message on the answering machine as follows: "You have reached . . . . *I* am not able to take your call right now. Leave a message and *I* will return your call as soon as *I* can." First of all, it assumed that the caller knew who "I" was, and second, totally disregarded the possibility that the caller might want to speak to another member of the household.

There are ways in which you can communicate a personal intent without overusing *I*. You might begin a sentence with "It seems to me," or "It has been my experience that . . ." or "My feeling is . . ."

Here's an alarming fact: of approximately eight hundred thousand words in the English language, we use about eight hundred on a regular basis. Those eight hundred words have fourteen thousand meanings. By division there are about seventeen meanings per word. In other words, we have a one-in-seventeen chance of being understood as we intended. Perhaps you've heard of Chisholm's Third Law—*If you explain something so clearly that no one can misunderstand, someone will.*

Again, this is where listening to yourself comes in. Be mindful of matching as closely as possible your words to your thoughts. Sometimes a short rehearsal on the way to an important meeting is a good way to hear back what you intend to say. Keep the number of words to a minimum. Outline the main issues in your mind or on paper. Weigh every word cautiously and check your listener periodically to see whether he is perceiving you correctly. Eliminate foggy words or phrases such as, "It is my determination that Johnny is demonstrating indicators of increased positive socialization with various classmates and his teachers," and replace them with "Johnny is getting along better with others." This word-by-word or phrase-by-phrase evaluation is particularly necessary when the discussion is complex or emotionally charged. As an extra check, encourage your listener to tell back or paraphrase your message to be sure it was delivered as you intended. These three steps—rehearsing, self-evaluating, and rechecking—can make you reasonably sure that you connected with your listener.

You must also be aware of comments or vocalizations that send a message you do not intend. For example, to some, nodding or saying "Uh-huh" suggests agreement. To others it simply means, "I am paying attention." There is no single universal interpretation of body movements or facial expressions. As our towns and workplaces become more culturally diverse, you must not expect people of different nationalities to respond nonverbally in the same way you do. A head nod in one culture (Japanese, for example), means, "I'm following you." In India, the same nod indicates disagreement.

Gestures and voice inflection should serve to *emphasize* and *reinforce* key words or phrases. These help the listener identify the important points, almost like using a highlighter pen to help you remember main ideas on a page.

In chapter four, I described silent negative self-talk as a barrier to attending to the listener. How about when you are the speaker? Making negative comments about yourself aloud in the company of others is double trouble. You must listen for these self-defeating remarks—even ask a friend to catch you in the act. You may cultivate very carefully other aspects of your image—wardrobe, punctuality, resume—so why in the world would you want to broadcast your inefficiencies? Every negative statement you make about yourself to others is instantly accepted as truth.

For example, Jim accidentally reads the wrong column on a document at an early meeting. He exclaims to the group, "Oh boy, I guess I'm not awake yet." Or upon misplacing an item, you may hear yourself announce, "I'd lose my head if it wasn't attached." These comments, meant to be excuses for your errors, seriously undermine your image and create a divide between yourself and exactly the persons with whom you are trying to develop a successful relationship.

To rid yourself of this self-defeating behavior, begin by becoming aware and extinguishing the silent negative self-talk (as described in chapter four). In situations where you find yourself in error or momentarily disorganized, excuse yourself and get back on track with the discussion. If you cannot locate an important document immediately or if your facts are incorrect, let others know you will locate the item ASAP or make the needed changes. *Period.* Avoid disparaging comments about yourself—no matter how badly you messed up.

Listen to yourself during informal group chit-chat. Do you speak negatively of others? Do you hear yourself gossiping or unfairly criticizing someone's appearance or berating someone's actions? You may be doing this to make yourself look better, yet this kind of talk only reinforces your status or prejudicial barriers. Instead of putting yourself in a positive light, you appear distrustful and insecure. Start by excusing yourself from those people-bashing sessions at the outset, and you will be on your way to eliminating a major adversary to mindful listening.

How often do you put your ego aside and sincerely compliment another? The proportion of negative to positive comments we make each day is startling. Once while waiting for my car to be fixed, I overheard about six different conversations between managers and their staff. After several minutes of listening to uncomplimentary and discouraging talk sprinkled with an occasional, "Thank you," or "Fine, thanks," I began a tally. Over a twenty-five-minute period I counted thirty-seven disparaging comments—and only two compliments or encouraging comments. The odd thing was that this dealership had a decent reputation and was fairly successful. I'd hate to be around if business got slow. The more I thought about it, the more I realized that these proportions are not unusual.

Is it any wonder we leave work discouraged? Why put in 200 percent on the job when no one really appreciates it? If we could hear ourselves as others do, we might be able to understand why staff turnover is high, why our kids avoid our company, or why our marriages get stale. Interestingly, we often think positive things about people but don't often let them know it. Why?

Many psychologists would say that we are too busy beating ourselves up with negative self-talk to give someone else a boost. If you begin balancing out negative self-talk with positive self-talk (suggested back in chapter four), it may be easier for you to vocalize positive comments about others. If you are compassionate with yourself, you'll more likely be compassionate toward others.

Sincere compliments like, "Hey, Gary, great job on that presentation!" or "Oh, Susan, that extra copy came in handy at the meeting today," or "Jenny, I really appreciate how you kept the noise down while I spoke with Mr. Smith," brighten up an ordinary afternoon. To forget yourself and your own neediness and let others know how they helped you out, performed well, or just plain did a good day's work will make you feel better about yourself.

It is very common to use preemptive comments like, "Excuse me, I know you must be very busy right now but . . ." or "You might not agree with me, but . . ." instead of getting right to the point. This kind of remark screams inferiority and insignificance rather than courtesy or respect. You probably make these tag remarks around certain people to whom you feel inferior—exactly the people you hope to impress. By getting to the point in a respectful rather than an obsequious manner, you establish a more symmetrical and productive relationship.

Tone and inflection carry their own sets of messages. An air of tentativeness is communicated when you make a question out of a declarative statement. "My first priority is to address the late-delivery issue?" or "The Jones account is a very important one?" indicate either a lack of confidence or a patronizing attitude.

I recall an administrator speaking like this to me when I was new to management. Perhaps she was trying to be motherly, but I found it condescending, as if she were checking that I comprehended her instructions, when she said things like, "Be sure to drop off your monthly statistics in my office?" However, she did the same thing in social situations, as in "I'm really glad I have a dog?" or "I felt it was the right thing to do?" This habitual rising inflection suggested ambivalence and created confusion. Listen carefully to the tone of your statements. Be sensitive to the reactions of your listeners. If you are perceived as indecisive or if people are continually questioning your stand on an issue, you may be asking for it.

Even more difficult to pay attention to are speakers who lack any inflection and lecture in a monotone. To those of you with these problems, I recommend voice therapy or a drama coach. Most of the time these vocal habits can be significantly improved. The hardest part is to listen objectively to the way you express yourself. The satisfying part is taking the steps to change.

Last but not least, listeners cringe at the sound of a voice that is too high pitched and nasal. Men are particularly irritated by women whose voices become shrill when they get excited or upset. When men get upset their pitch also rises, but not to levels that annoy the ear. Women's voices are usually about an octave higher to begin with, so when some females speak under stress, their voices often soar to much higher levels.

Hold Your Tongue

1. If you are a chronic interrupter, halt your interruption midsentence and say, "Excuse me. Please go on with what you were saying." In time, you will catch yourself *before* you interrupt. However, if from the start of the conversation you get into their movie, your focus will not be on your agenda anyway; you will be totally absorbed with understanding your speakers, and there will be less tendency for you to interrupt.

2. As a speaker, there are acceptable ways to stave off an interrupter. Watch some of the political group discus-

sions on CNN to learn the technique. When someone jumps in on you to disagree or to dominate the conversation, hold up your index finger, signaling "Just a minute," and continue talking. If the verbal intruder persists, stop and say, "Let me finish and then I will listen to you." Continue with what you were saying. Be mindful that the speaker may have a practical reason for interrupting (i.e., you are out of time; there is an important call for you).

3. If *you* need to interrupt for a legitimate reason, raise a hand to chest level and address the person by name. "Bob, excuse me, but due to time, we must get back on track," or "Linda, we are out of time." Using their names gets their attention.

4. The next time you have to give a talk or present an issue, find a private place and tape yourself on video or audio. It is often astounding to hear yourself as your listeners will hear you. Reflect on your choice of words, tone of voice, and other aspects of your presentation. You may well want to revise a few things. (By the way, your voice sounds different on tape. Most of us are familiar with our voices as they reverberate through our skulls. The recorded voice is very close to the sound that other people hear.)

5. In our quest to become compassionate listeners, "friendly" is a good place to start. Come up with a new, friendlier greeting for your voice mail. Avoid the robotic phrases you hear on everyone else's voice mail like, "I'm either on the phone, or . . ." No kidding! Smile as you

speak, as if you just received a great compliment from your boss. Now listen with the ears of a stranger. Does it make you smile or feel welcomed? In the words of Jeffrey Gitomer, author of *Customer Satisfaction Is Worthless, Customer Loyalty Is Priceless*, "Friendly makes sales—and friendly generates repeat business."

6 .To combat frequent swearing, practice using more acceptable expletives. Brainstorm a variety of synonyms to describe a person, situation, or anything else to which you might reflexively attach the swear word. For example, instead of saying, "That was the best f——— cheesecake I ever ate," you might substitute "most delectable" or "exquisite."

7. To practice choosing words carefully, take a piece of paper and draw an abstract design. Find a partner and give him a piece of paper and a pen. With your design visible only to yourself, describe the shapes and locations on the paper as clearly as possible. See if your partner interprets your words as you intended and reproduces the design exactly.

8. Look for the subtle negatives in your habitual responses and turn them into positives. For example, if you are the appointment scheduler, you may find yourself in a *rut response pattern,* saying things like, "I'm sorry there's nothing open for you till next week." That comment makes others feel unwanted and disappointed. If there's nothing you can do to create the desired time slot, try making the

same message positive: "Mr. Jones, you're in luck! Dr. Smith has an opening next Friday!"

9. Below is a list of negative responses. Keep the same message but make your listener feel good.

- We won't have any more size twelves until Monday.

- Get in line with everyone else.

- You're really lost aren't you? Where's your map?

- You can't be serious about fixing this bike.

- Mr. Ramirez is waiting to get an important call. Call back later.

- Our new computer system has lost your file. Try back tomorrow.

Here are some suggested answers:

- Every Monday we get in a large shipment, including size twelves. May I put something aside for you next Monday?

- To be fair to those who have been waiting, we need to make a line.

- I'll help you get back home. Do you have a map, by any chance?

- I'm really sorry, but this bike can't be repaired.

- Mr. Ramirez is eager to speak with you, but he is helping another customer right now. May he call you back in a few minutes?

- Today we're having some computer difficulties. I apologize for the inconvenience.

Chapter Nine

Listening Under Stress

Loyalty to a petrified opinion never yet broke a chain or freed a human soul.

—Mark Twain

 p to this point we have discussed listening in rather peaceful conditions—lectures, friendly conversations, meetings, and so on—where facts and figures are received without much emotional turmoil. When good or neutral feelings exist between you and the speaker, it is much easier to meet your listening objectives.

However, when a listening situation is uncomfortable, our ability to listen usually breaks down. Stressful listening situations may cover a broad range of circumstances. Aside from full-blown arguments and disciplinary events, they may also include job interviews, counseling sessions, talking to the boss, negotiation, getting directions from a stranger, or meeting new people. Your practice thus far has prepared you for better listening in these latter situations. Your improved ability to put aside your agenda, process information more accurately, and get into the movie of the speaker eliminates most of the anxiety associated with these situations. Your continued practice will make them even easier.

During heated arguments and confrontations, the listening demands are much greater. The challenge is to process not only the words and emotions behind the words, but to avoid becoming defensive and/or eventually offensive. To do this you need to *unconditionally accept* the reality of the other person as legitimate. You need to remain calm and focused in order to choose your words carefully. You can see how listening under stress is the ultimate test of the firmness of your foundation for mindful listening.

Interestingly, in my listening class, this listening-under-stress segment is very popular. Stressful listening situations are commonplace in our society. The pressures of school and the workplace are brought home and added to the mix of family problems. In these forum discussions, my students become very open and uninhibited about how their listening abilities break down when conflict arises. Many of us find it uncomfortable to disagree openly or make critical observations. One reason for this is concern about how the other person will take it.

Perhaps in the past your difference of opinion was not welcomed or the other person's reaction was threatening to you or the relationship. So now you prefer to nod, be nice, and agree with the opposing point of view while your true feelings fester. At that point you run up against a wall of self-recrimination that serves only to reinforce negative self-talk.

How can you start to feel comfortable when listening under stress and break this cycle of frustration? Before you can listen well in stressful encounters you must be able to

- recognize your barriers and work through the ones you can change. ("Ah-ha! Here comes George. I'm starting to cringe just thinking about his comments at last week's meeting. But

I'm going to try to keep an open mind and avoid getting bogged down by the past.");

- be able to put aside your agenda and get into the movie of the other in order to understand where he is coming from;

- be able to relax by controlling your breathing;

- have a genuine interest in establishing a positive relationship.

For centuries, the greatest martial artists, well equipped with weapons and fighting skills, have said that it is always best to avoid conflict in the first place. However, sometimes conflict is unavoidable, as in a self-defense situation. In the martial arts, the objective is not to kill the aggressor, but to put him in a situation where he is no longer a threat. Effective self-defense maneuvers require sharp mental focus; physical strength is secondary. Without practice in breath control, just the opposite occurs—your mental focus breaks down and you become more physically tense.

When you are fearful, your strength increases by at least 20 percent due to the strong rush of adrenaline. The liver demands more oxygen from the heart and lungs as it pumps sugar into the bloodstream. As a result of the blood supply being diverted to the extremities (the fight-or-flight response), the blood supply to the problem-solving part of the brain is significantly reduced. Similar to a martial artist, you need to maintain sharp mental focus to avoid becoming defensive and verbally provocative, which only intensify emotions. That is why breathing practice is such a major part of martial arts training and why I promote it as a basic skill for listening.

If stressful interactions are common in your home and workplace, try to identify the patterns of behavior that trigger them. Quite often you may be the recipient of someone's displaced anger, and the fact that you just happen to be in the same room is enough to spark a conflict. Other times, you may create situations that invite conflict. Purposefully bringing up the name of an old girlfriend, pointing out someone's bad habits, or rarely having anything positive to say could be the hot buttons for stopping the listening process. Unfortunately, the better you know someone, the better you know what irks her and how to get a reaction.

An insensitive response style or letting your barriers into the discussion also fuels the fire of conflict. If you are the guilty party, you are aware of and somewhat in control of these behaviors. But for some, due to psychological problems or a history of abuse, it may be very difficult to repress or eliminate them. If past issues chronically play havoc with your communications with others, psychological counseling may be called for. Yet many disagreements that incite stressful interactions with family or workmates can be resolved by acknowledging your barriers, trying to understand the disgruntled other, and connecting with your breath.

I make a point of staying in touch with students who take my class, particularly those who have had a hard time listening under stress. Some of them have very moody spouses or bosses. Others live with emotionally disturbed family members. After taking my class, these students report instant awareness of their barriers when interacting with these difficult persons. They admit saying to themselves and others, "He's been angry all week; why should today be different?" or "Here comes that nasty old Mrs. Hastings. Every time I see her coming I know she's going to complain about something!" Inevitably the interaction goes sour—just as the listener planned it! Now, when they peer into what makes these people act the way they do (get into their movie), the feelings transform from extreme dislike to curiosity, making room for empathy and compassion.

This perspective softens your reaction, and keeps you from becoming defensive in the face of adversity. Incidentally, compassion does not mean pity or sympathy; it means getting a sense of the other person's frustration. *Com* means "to connect with," and *passion* means "suffering." The Dalai Lama defines compassion in practical terms: "Compassion is a sense of responsibility. Compassion is wanting to share with others. We all have responsibility to shape the future of humanity. So (by being compassionate) let us try to contribute as much as we can."

The philosopher Martin Buber might also have been describing compassion when he suggested that you listen until you experience the other side of the argument. Make it your responsibility to understand the other side by getting into the movie of the other person. Dr. Richard Cabot described this experience when he said, "We do not understand an opposing idea *until we have so exposed ourselves to it that we feel the pull of its persuasion,* until we arrive at the point where we really see the power of whatever element of truth it contains" (emphasis added).

What makes us think that the only people we can effectively work and live with are people similar to ourselves? We make life more difficult when we avoid those who differ from us. Especially in our culturally and religiously diverse society, making a point to avoid interaction with those from different backgrounds shuts us off from seeing different perspectives on a problem and reduces our capacity for creative solutions. Making a point of interacting only with those who are like us creates *mental narrowing.* Many poor listeners are inflexible thinkers and resist ideas that bend the rules or break the mold. For these persons, advice giving and denial are the preferred modes of verbal communication; it's their way or the highway. Forcing our ideas on others merely escalates conflict.

In the workplace, poor listening limits productivity in many ways. First, it discourages information sharing that could make a product or service more desirable or enable employees to get more done in less time. Poor listening creates a desert where otherwise a forest of ideas would flourish. When a free flow of ideas is stymied, energy and enthusiasm are squelched, resulting in lost sales, poor quality, and costly mistakes.

From a Zen perspective, interpersonal conflict can be a means of personal growth. Of course, peace and harmony are preferable to anger and discontent, but if you recall from earlier chapters, strong preferences often get us into trouble by reinforcing barriers. Therefore, as unthinkable as it may seem in an angry moment, let's try looking for that golden nugget or the seed of opportunity for growth hidden deep within a stressful listening situation.

Professor Richard Walton, in his book *Interpersonal Peacemaking: Confrontations and Third-Part Consultation,* pointed out some constructive benefits of conflict, applicable to boardroom, bedroom, and classroom. Walton claims that dealing with conflict helps you see better into your own position. Having to articulate your needs in response to another's needs allows you to question the rationality of your own arguments. You may decide after all that something is not worth arguing about. You may have a weak supporting argument or no real support for your position. Perhaps there is a deeper issue underlying this surface problem. If you are the one responsible for inciting the argument, mindfulness may give you the courage to explore your internal conflicts.

Last, conflict can spur innovative approaches to problems. Especially when there is a diversity of needs and viewpoints and a heightened sense of necessity, motivation and energy are high. This chemistry releases creative potential for problem solving. As the philosopher John Dewey wrote, "Conflict is the *sin qua non* of reflection and ingenuity." Thomas Crum, in his book *The Magic of Conflict,* suggests that we see conflict in a positive light in which neither side loses and a new dance is created. He points out that Nature uses conflict as a primary motivator for the creation of beautiful beaches, canyons, mountains, and pearls. Being able to listen well in conflict, according to Crum, begins by unhitching the burden of belief systems (barriers) that prevent us from appreciating our differences.

Let's take a common example in which Mary, a not-so-favorite co-worker, is promoted as your new manager. If you remain rigid in your perception of this new arrangement, your knee-jerk response may be denial, anger, or resentment. You may even consider looking for another job or going to a new department—anything to avoid Mary. Here is an example of superficial thought processes that focus on the concrete aspects of this relationship. Notice how surface thinking drags negative self-talk into the process:

- Mary has never taken my knowledge and experience seriously. *This won't change.*

- Mary is *younger* than I am. *I can't deal* with these new-wave approaches.

- Mary's background is administration; *she doesn't understand* field work.

The other option is to stay in your present job and take on the challenge of understanding what divides you and Mary. (These same issues usually follow us from job to job anyway.) You can begin by pinpointing the barriers that separate you and Mary. These may include age, race, gender, past experiences, or a host of others. Now look at the source of these barriers. What you may see is an overwhelming focus on your self-interests and a lack of concern for the big picture. Perhaps you are fearful of comparison or not being included in key meetings. Ask yourself: Why do I feel this way about myself? Is there any basis for my fears? Has this happened before? If yes, did I take the steps necessary to turn these weaknesses into strengths?

The answers may make you uncomfortable, but at least you recognized that your agenda and status are major barriers in effectively interacting with Mary. At this point, you can choose to remain stuck in the mud with this attitude and make your life miserable, or you can perceive the situation from a more creative and flexible point of view.

Are there any points on which you and Mary agree? Can you find balance between your experience and what Mary has to offer? How could you and she together turn a potentially disagreeable arrangement into a positive team effort? Shifting the focus from yourself to the big picture is the next step toward personal growth.

As much as it may physically and mentally tax you to accept this challenge, it is possible that you, the company, and your coworkers may derive long-term benefit from this arrangement. Hence, you have established the mindset of the flexible thinker—one who is willing to consider a range of alternatives to reduce potential stresses with Mary. Your list might look something like this:

- Mary and I have had a rocky past, but perhaps we can put that behind us and see how we can meet today's challenges.

- Perhaps getting some fresh ideas will spur us to brainstorm as a group; after all, the old routines don't seem to be working.

- Maybe if I had a better understanding of the administrative side of things, I would be able to provide customers with more answers. This knowledge would make me feel more confident in my job.

Look for the synergy between you and Mary. Perhaps you and she are more compatible coworkers than you think. Mary may appreciate your independent approach to things, but it could also be necessary for you to become more of a team player. Would this challenge not benefit you? Can you imagine (and I recommend that you try visualizing a similar situation during breathing practice) a relaxed and fruitful conversation about how the team can best achieve its goals for the coming year, or brainstorming ways of raising money for a project? Just as you can shape the outcome of your meeting with Mrs. Hastings and create stress, you have the power to create a stress-free and potentially creative situation with your new boss.

If you are going to meet with someone and you anticipate difficulties, try dissecting the problem in its spark stage instead of allowing the chain reaction of emotions to reach an explosion. I described this process in chapter four as a way of using meditation to dissolve the emotions associated with barriers. Matthieu Ricard describes how to break down potential anxieties that cause us so much suffering. He suggests that we

> . . . grasp the nature of thoughts and trace them to their very source. A feeling of hatred, for example, can seem extremely solid and powerful, and can create a sort of knot somewhere in our chests and completely change the way we behave. But if we look at it we see that it is not brandishing any weapon, it can't crush us like a boulder could or burn us like a fire. In reality the whole thing began with a tiny thought, which has gradually grown and swollen up like a storm cloud. From far away, summer clouds can look very impressive and solid. You really feel you could sit on them. But when you get inside them there's hardly anything there. They turn out to be completely intangible. In the same way, when we look at a thought and trace it back to its source, we can't find anything substantial. At that moment the thought evaporates. This is called "liberating thoughts by looking at their nature," meaning to recognize their "emptiness." Once we've liberated a thought, it won't set off a chain reaction. Instead it'll dissolve without a trace, like a bird flying through the sky.

I've tried this approach successfully several times with issues that troubled me, both personal and professional. Once I was called into the vice president's office to defend my proposal for a major project at the hospital. I was given several days to prepare; this also gave me sufficient time to build up a storm cloud of anxiety over it. From the moment the meeting was called, the knot in my chest started to ache, so I tried to liberate it before it got worse. I traced the anxious feelings to my fears: 1) losing my job, being replaced by someone who commanded a lower salary, 2) the job-seeking process, 3) disappointing my family and causing them worry, 4) the possibility of having to relocate, and 5) not being persuasive enough.

I discovered that at the heart of all these fears was an ego that felt threatened. My list did not include more critical issues like whether or not I would be able to pay my bills. It all had to do with facing the possibility of a major change and losing face. I chuckled to myself. The knot in my chest was loosening already. This wasn't such a big problem after all. Sure, I'd like to keep my job, but the possibility of moving out west had always been exciting. I could get my chance! This meeting might be a disguise for a new opportunity! I was prepared to defend the proposal; I knew I had done my best. Now I was no longer dreading the meeting, I was only curious to see where it led.

The reason that listening well under stress seems, at first, so daunting is that when we hear something unsettling, our thinking turns inward. We become preoccupied with ourselves. We see the issue as inseparable from our emotions. Stepping back to determine where these emotions are coming from helps loosen their grip on the psyche.

Linda, a student from my class, successfully applied this tracing-back approach when her son announced that he was planning to drop out of college. He felt stifled by academic life and saw more opportunities outside the college environment. He wanted to seek out these opportunities and perhaps return to school at some later time. Linda's reaction was shock and anger. Tracing back her reaction to her son's announcement, she realized how attached she was to conventional barriers: the perceptions of her friends and what they would say about her as a mother, her son labeled a dropout, jealousy that her friends would see their sons graduate and she wouldn't. Linda faced the barriers of status, negative self-talk, and wanting to control her son's choices. She acknowledged that these barriers were fears based on pride and ego. Of course, Linda remained disappointed with her son's decision, but by discovering the source of her turmoil, she was able to diffuse her reactions to the point of caring more about her son's present unhappiness and his optimism for the future. Linda was free to get into his movie and understand her son better.

We can't expect ourselves to ignore feelings of anger, resentment, or fear that present as obstacles to hearing someone out. Yet we can search for the source of these feelings, and quite often it is our egos expressing greed or hatred for some person or idea. Let's say you are very angry with your brother for something he said to your parents, and you are about to have a conversation with him. Beforehand, get to the source of the bad feelings you have toward your brother. How realistic is it to expect that you can protect your parents from insults and hurtful situations? If you show anger toward your brother, will he be any more sensitive to your parents? If the answer to these questions is "no," you have begun to face the source of your negative feelings. You are not denying your anger; you still feel bad for your parents, but you have separated yourself from a situation you cannot change. Just like in dealing with our negative self-talk in chapter four, let a positive thought or idea cancel out a negative one. Neutralize your anger by thinking of an admirable trait or some positive action your brother demonstrated. Try to wish him well instead of wishing him ill. If you find this difficult, it may mean that you are still battling with your own negative self-talk. Before you can be compassionate with others, you have to be compassionate with yourself.

Mindful listening under stress begins inside and works outward.

Another student, Karen, a marketing representative for a large pharmaceutical company, came to my class because she felt uncomfortable with networking. She was getting pressure from her boss to participate in activities that would draw in more business. Despite the many opportunities she lost as a result of not attending networking functions, the thought of having to "shmooze" with strangers was stressful. Karen had even considered changing careers.

When I asked Karen what she disliked about networking, she reported that she felt she had to act a certain way—overly friendly, insincere, witty, and animated. Because of her nervousness with her self-imposed pressure to perform, she was rarely able to walk away with any usable information; therefore, networking was a waste of time. Karen admitted that there was a lot of negative self-talk going on in her head, and she agreed to work on that problem until our next meeting. Shortly after completing the listening class, she began meditating. She became more comfortable with silence, plus there was a lot less negative noise going on in her head. At that point, Karen began getting into the movies of friends and family members. She started to experience freedom from her self-consciousness. She could listen mindfully to others and put her own mind traffic aside for longer and longer periods of time.

Karen began to experience listening as an adventure. She claimed, "The more I put my agenda aside, the more I can sense the whole message coming through." Karen enthusiastically accepted her next networking invitation. Afterward, she reported that "time flew by." She didn't feel the pressure to perform because she cast the spotlight on her speaker instead of herself. By giving of herself in this way, Karen got more than she had bargained for: repeat business and word-of-mouth referrals, much to the pleasure of her boss. She formed new contacts, better understood her competition, and made a few relationships with customers that had long-term potential. Karen now teaches mindful networking skills to her staff.

Those who choose not to be so rigid about people and things, seeing all approaches as necessary for the balance of the common good, turn out to be the best listeners. For some of us, a change in mindset may be sufficient, but for the majority of us, a consensus between mind and body is necessary to take on such a challenge. Never before have we been exposed to such high levels of anxiety in our everyday lives. Global concerns about AIDS and other mysterious viruses, drug addiction, wide swings in the economy, and threats of terrorism top the list. Then there are the garden varieties of anxiety that we bring on ourselves—extreme attachment to material wealth, obsessions with weight and dieting, procrastination, the need for instant gratification—that have rerouted our consciousness. The alienation brought on by a thriving economy, a skyrocketing stock market, explosive technological innovation, and instant wealth creates an unprecedented amount of stress. Philosopher Peter Koestenbaum refers to the "new-economy pathology" as the affliction imposed by the need to meet ever-higher objectives in all realms of work, wealth, and lifestyle. "A terrible insensitivity to basic human values," Koestenbaum warns, is the result of placing emphasis on the price of a stock over what it really means to be a successful human being (*Fast Company*, March 2000).

Understanding the different kinds of anxiety helps us know which need managing and which are conducive to personal growth. In addition, different people will experience different degrees of listener anxiety depending on the situation and their genetic predisposition.

Robert Gerzon, in his book *Finding Serenity in the Age of Anxiety*, describes three different kinds of anxiety:

- *Natural anxiety* (the good anxiety) acts as a warning mechanism, but also alerts us to moments of opportunity. The theme of natural anxiety is "just do it." I compare it to a level of mental energy needed to focus on a challenging and enjoyable task.

- *Ontological* (or existential) *anxiety* is born of grappling with issues of the purpose of life and life after death and is related to a heightened need to answer questions about our existence.

- *Toxic anxiety* arises from the refusal to face the other two. Instead of acknowledging natural anxiety and ontological anxiety as necessary and appropriate, we ignore them, with the result that they fester into a poisonous mental state. Freud called this *neurotic anxiety,* the kind of mental dysfunction that takes the form of depression, addiction, or mood disorders. It can become so extreme that it overwhelms our ability to listen and think clearly. If unresolved, toxic anxiety leads to violence, alienation, and—eventually—to physical illness.

Natural and ontological anxiety are the most conducive to mindful listening. They imply a state of readiness and hunger for knowledge, both prerequisites for attending to and concentrating on the message. However, extremes of natural and ontological anxiety can lead to toxic states. Obsessive type-A personalities or religious zealots are familiar examples. Unless these types learn to channel their anxieties toward positive achievement and spiritual growth, they may plummet to the depths of frustration and paranoia.

Negative self-talk, mentioned earlier as a major barrier to listening, is an internal source of anxiety. It creates an inner noise that foils our attempts to listen effectively. We overreact to these thoughts, real or imagined, causing our blood pressure to rise and our normal bodily functions—breathing, digesting, and speaking—to become dysfunctional. Negative self-talk subverts the mind-body balance needed to think clearly and act effectively, particularly in stressful encounters.

Look back on a recent situation in which you were verbally confronted. Perhaps it was an angry boss, spouse, or child. What did you do as they ranted and raved? Chances are, your body was tense, you had to swallow hard, and you felt yourself blushing. You might have thought negatively of yourself and even more negatively toward the person shouting at you. Perhaps you started thinking about the consequences of this verbal attack—would you be fired, divorced, ignored? All the while, this noise in your brain prevented you from taking that first positive step toward a successful resolution—focusing on the issue. Say it was a personal accusation, such as "You are always fifteen to twenty minutes late!" The real issue is that in that span of time, the business loses out on ten calls that could generate hundreds of dollars in revenue. You have the choice to perceive this as a personal attack or you can see the complaint as a functional problem that affects the whole system: *the company is losing out on so many calls; this affects everybody in the group. There must be a way to plan ahead so I can get to my desk by eight o'clock.* The former response is anxiety producing, laden with barriers that prevent self-understanding and growth. The latter response focuses on the issue (missing valuable calls) and includes an action step. It is unrealistic to expect yourself to shut out feelings of anger and resentment when you are under attack, but you can put the issue in the foreground and the noise in the background. This way you can get on with *solving the problem*, which is the outcome both parties desire.

In *The Art of Happiness*, the Dalai Lama comments on how we tend to overreact to minor things and blow them out of proportion by endlessly recounting the situation, further feeding the anger and dislike. This is the way we create our own suffering and anxiety. He explains:

For example, say that you find out that someone is speaking badly of you behind your back. If you react to this knowledge that someone is speaking badly of you, this negativity, with a feeling of hurt or anger, then you yourself destroy your own peace of mind. Your pain is your own personal creation. On the other hand, if you let the slander pass by you as if it were a silent wind passing behind your ears, you protect yourself from that feeling of hurt, that feeling of agony. So although you may not always be able to avoid difficult situations you can modify the extent to which you suffer by how you choose to respond to the situation.

Similarly, in the art of *jiujitsu,* the way to defend against an opponent is to yield to the full force of the attack, but turn it in the opposite direction to avoid being harmed. Perhaps you have seen documentary films of martial-arts masters who demonstrate the ability to turn away an attacker by directing the negative energy back toward the aggressor with a calm eye and barely a flick of the wrist. It does not require years of martial-arts training to determine how great or how small a problem is. With a basic foundation in mindfulness, you can calmly evaluate the situation and judge to what extent you want to take your stress levels.

It requires a sense of calm in order to rationally deal with the onslaught of verbal conflict. In describing how matadors deal with a charging bull in the ring, Ernest Hemingway said in *Death in the Afternoon,* "To calmly watch the bull come is the most necessary and primarily difficult thing in bullfighting." Our tendency, when the bull or verbal aggressor is on the attack, is to interrupt, begin objecting, or leave the room. This only angers the charging other more, escalates bad feelings, and postpones a positive outcome. If you have any prior notice of an impending confrontation, prepare with a few deep, slow breaths and continue breathing slowly and fully as you listen.

Unsuccessful attempts to communicate under stress give you

the sense of a split between mind and body. Your breath gets out of control and your heart rate speeds up. Notice how your breath becomes shallow and how your shoulders and neck tense. The mind is on the defensive, erecting barriers and shooting words from the hip. Perhaps this state of intense discomfort is the reason we so dislike conflict and avoid it at all costs.

Regular breathing practice, *daily meditation on the breath,* helps restore balance and connection between mind and body. You can easily learn to revert from tight, shallow breathing to a deep abdominal breath, which relaxes the neck and shoulders. You may not see instant results, but over several days or a few short weeks the changes are apparent.

Meditation increases the brain's alpha waves, which elevate our sense of well-being. For centuries, Eastern cultures have promoted meditation as a means of attaining peace. Meditation practice helps you attain a sense of deep relaxation that allows you to step back and see situations in a clearer light, unobstructed by barriers and noise. This alert, calm state of mindfulness, achieved through regular practice, begins to permeate every interaction. Whenever you are teaching, consulting, conversing, or whatever your day brings, it is this deep relaxation that brings quality to the moment. You will begin to notice that situations that once would have caused an excessively emotional reaction are now resolved in a calmer, more productive manner.

If some of these suggestions for listening under stress are difficult for you to apply right now, try not to be discouraged. Continue to work on your foundation for being a mindful listener in more laid-back contexts. Your confidence in your ability to communicate with others will increase as you become more efficient and notice others responding to you more favorably. To consistently process auditory information accurately *under pressure* is the aim of even the best listeners!

Getting a head start in relaxation helps set your mind to focus on the issue at hand rather than the negative noise competing for your attention. As your conversation partner launches into her complaint, continue to keep your breath steady and slow. If you have practiced the relaxation exercises in chapter three, this should come easier to you. Withhold the temptation to interrupt and start defending yourself. Instead, encourage the speaker to tell you more. Ask questions like, "Is there anything else that has upset you?" or "What do you mean by slacking off?" Quite often the opening remarks are just the tip of the iceberg. The real issue is usually several minutes down the road.

Getting into their movie is crucial to being able to listen well in situations where someone you care about is under stress. The focus is not on yourself, but on seeing the other's viewpoint. Saying, "Is there anything else?" is the *last* thing a speaker expects to hear, and it signals that you are eager and receptive to solving the problem. In many cases, this request calms the waters. The speaker senses that she will not be interrupted and does not have to race against the clock. Her body relaxes and her volume drops down. Allowing those extra minutes for the speaker to verbalize her whole concern reduces the chances of another stressful encounter on the same topic days or weeks later. However, there are times when that invitation to speak her mind gives the speaker license to open the floodgates and bring up other issues unrelated or indirectly related to the topic at hand. This may give you more insight into the problem, i.e., a general discontent with life, not enough free time, problems at work, and so on. Just as with the silent response discussed in chapter seven, the speaker may, by hearing herself expound on the problem, arrive at her own solutions. If the speaker appears to be straying from the topic, it may be necessary to refocus on the main issue. Either way, asking the angry person to elaborate on her complaint helps get to the bottom of the problem.

Remember the power of silence? Sometimes people may start

off with what appears to be a trivial complaint. You may say to yourself, "How could he get so mad about me not dumping the garbage?" But this is often just a starting point. Keep eye contact and let him continue until he is finished. Watch your breath and keep it slow and steady. Pause for several seconds and *wait*. At that point, the person may sense that you are giving him the go-ahead to get to the heart of the problem. Or he may have truly finished and not dumping the garbage on a regular basis is the only issue. Either way, begin by briefly paraphrasing what was just said to you. Try to avoid sounding too clinical with phrases like, "So, what I hear you saying is . . ." or "So, to recap, what you're telling me is . . ." Be natural and remember why you are telling back what you heard—to better understand the speaker's point of view. Simply say, "I want to make sure I'm getting everything you are saying to me. Let me see if I understand . . ." Leave out foul language and dramatic imitations. This lets the speaker know you heard him and gives him a chance to amend inaccuracies. After you have paraphrased your understanding of what was said, ask for clarification. "Is my understanding of this problem correct?" You may ask questions to get more clarification. Then state your case briefly and to the point; then offer to brainstorm possible solutions. Listening to your words during stressful discussions is essential to avoid fueling the fire.

Whenever loved ones are angry and upset, our goal as listeners is to help them feel understood, not put down. Get into their movies. Being silently attentive is particularly helpful while listening to angry, upset children. If your child comes home complaining about something that a teacher said, you may be tempted to try to talk him out of his feelings, as if they are not to be taken seriously. If you can put your "shoulds," interrogation, and advice aside and instead remain silently attentive, your child will feel safe about revealing his emotions. If you still feel pressed to give your advice, wait until he has finished all he has to say. Then you might say, "Would you like to hear what I might have done if I had been in your shoes?" If he wants to know, let him ask.

Try to avoid cross-complaining. ("You say *I* never take out the garbage? Well, *you* never do the laundry!") Avoid using absolutes like *never, always,* and *every*. Absolutes and *should* are hot-button words that can easily shut down your partner's willingness to listen.

When someone is yelling at you, keep your voice soft and steady, just like your breath. This voice response can be very helpful in quieting your partner's voice. It is often difficult for us to listen to swearing and other expletives delivered in a loud, hostile tone. Our bodies naturally tense in response to threatening behavior. But, just like the matador, we will most certainly lose the battle if our fight-or-flight tendency takes over.

Agree with what you can. There may be something you both can agree on, such as, "You are right about that. I don't take out the garbage most nights. But this is because I don't think of it. I'll try to pay more attention." The issue may well be that you don't follow through on household responsibilities. If that is the case, try to treat this as an *issue,* not an attack. By this time, your adversary may be calming down too. He was given the chance to say all that was bothering him. He sees that there is no need to continue screaming, because by paraphrasing, you have shown that you truly listened (you care). Now he feels, even in a small way, indebted to listen to you. At this point you have set the stage for a successful negotiation of the problem.

There may be times when it is not appropriate to continue the discussion. You may not be in a good mood, the setting may not be conducive, or time is a factor. In that case, ask to continue the discussion at another time, preferably that day. This shows good faith and gives you an opportunity to set the stage for a more positive outcome.

There are certain individuals who, due to lack of emotional and physical control, make it unsafe and unreasonable to get into their movies. With persons who pose a danger to you, emotionally or physically, it may be best to leave the room or remain silent. The last thing you need to get from these people is more. They may require a combination of psychological counseling and restraint. You may have to seek guidance for special ways of dealing with these dangerous individuals.

A mindful listener sees all interactions as equal. Pleasant conversations reinforce a positive relationship and hold promise for future interactions. Conflict poses opportunities; the process of working through conflict contributes more to personal growth than the resolution itself. If you look to the less desirable relationships or contacts in your life as an opportunity for achieving balance between mind and body, you will not find yourself wanting to hide your head in the sand when conflict arises. This attitude takes the stress out of the discussion. If your purpose is to resolve the issue to the extent where all parties are satisfied—versus winning the argument—you may become less resistant to situations where opinions differ. When there is less emphasis on the outcome and more emphasis on the process of listening, a relationship is established.

Did you ever think of a complaint by a customer or disgruntled other as code for "I want to continue a relationship with you/your company, but something is amiss"? Try to see complaints as coming from a concerned individual who wants things to go smoother between you. If salvaging the relationship were not the case, she would have ceased contact. A complaint is an opportunity to set things right.

Allowing silence, getting into her movie, paraphrasing her complaint, are perceived by the disgruntled other as action steps in restoring the relationship; they act as the cornerstone for future resolutions. Take the anxiety out of listening in difficult situations by seeing them as a challenge to your personal growth.

Hardiness, a term coined by Salvatore Maddi and Suzanne

Kobasa, describes the tendency of certain individuals to respond to threatening situations by transforming them into manageable challenges. Thich Nhat Hahn says, "In Zen everything one does becomes a vehicle for self-realization, every act, every movement is done wholeheartedly with nothing left over."

A note to those of you who work in the customer complaint office: try this exercise and finish each day with a sense of accomplishment instead of burnout. Using the suggestions above for listening under stress, keep a count each day of how many unhappy customers you turned into happy customers. Set a quota and inspire others in your department to do the same. Call back the most disgruntled customers as soon as possible to let them know you followed up on their complaints or changes in their service. Because you listen, they will reward you with continued business and new referrals because they know you cared.

Let Stress Be Your Teacher

1. Relaxed attentiveness is a necessary first step. Stay true to your daily breathing practice. Meditate about twenty minutes twice a day (if you can) every day for a week. Find a quiet spot, sit up tall, relax your eyes (eyelids closed or half-open) and breathe slowly. Focus only on how your breath moves in and out of your body. Other thoughts may enter your consciousness, but let them pass and refocus on the breath. It may be helpful to count the breaths silently if focusing on just the movement of the breath is difficult. (For specific guidelines, please see Eknath Easwaran's book, *Meditation.*)

If you find thoughts about a particular person or an upcoming event interfering with your practice, take a few minutes to make this situation manageable. Relax and close your eyes, breathe for a few minutes, and settle yourself. Think of pleasant, relaxing experiences, like sitting by a campfire, fishing on a quiet lake, sipping tea, or listening to music. Notice how you feel void of any tension in your body. After a few minutes, start to think of communication interactions that make you mildly self-conscious or intimidated. Begin by seeing the positive traits of this person or situation. See yourself reacting calmly. See the interaction going smoothly—standing tall, arms relaxed, feeling confident, able to converse fluently. Breathe through these thoughts at the same relaxed pace you started with. See yourself relaxed and calm. See yourself not doing the things that created negative outcomes in the past, such as interrupting, use of absolutes, or cross-complaining. See yourself listening attentively, fully in the speaker's movie, with good eye contact and a composed posture. Avoid feelings of criticism or defensiveness. If any negative thoughts creep into your scenario or if you feel your body tense, get back on track by checking your breathing—slow and steady. Go back to the beginning until you can see a calm response to whatever is said, from start to finish. See the interaction ending successfully with good feelings on both sides. Think about how much you both accomplished. Continue easy breathing for a few more minutes, savoring the process by which you accomplished this result. Gradually open your eyes and go make that appointment!

2. Be empathetic with another's view on a controversial subject. Find a friend who will try this exercise with you. Pick a topic over which you disagree. Take turns defending your friend's viewpoint; enthusiastically develop your argument. After this exercise, do you still feel as convinced of your original point of view? Is it a little easier to listen to an opposing viewpoint on other topics?

3. Before dealing with a personal conflict, plan your discussion on paper. Without too much attention to structure and neatness, write out key ideas and sentences as they come to you. Now look at what you wrote and edit out the vague, rambling portions. Will your listener immediately understand your intent and get the message? Clarify your thoughts, review your word choice, and cut it down to size. Notice how much more direct and effective your message is.

4. When a customer makes a complaint, let him finish and then respond on a positive note, with:

- That's my favorite problem!

- I'm sure we can find a way.

- Consider that taken care of!

- I will try to get an answer for you as fast as I can.

- Thank you for bringing that to my attention!

Conclude with a tell-me-more: "Is there anything else I can help you with today?"

Chapter Ten

Boosting Your Listening Memory

A good listener is not only popular everywhere,
but after a while, he knows something.

—Wilson Mizner

In almost every listening class I teach there are a handful of people who think that they are losing it—because they have become scattered or absentminded. Mindlessness, if allowed to go wild, fragments our attention with the result that many minutes and hours in our lives go unnoticed. When our thoughts are scattered somewhere in the past or future, our minds are absent from the present reality. This kind of suffering creates needless havoc in our lives and makes us feel inadequate and stupid.

Mindfulness practice helps us to reassemble our dispersed attention, restore concentration, and build self-esteem. To attain mindfulness requires regular application, but most importantly, it takes a sustained commitment to do away with *mindlessness*. It often helps to have a vision of the kind of listener you want to be—calm, focused, and able to process and remember whatever you choose.

Now that you have invested some time in self-awareness and regular breathing practice, it is time to apply mindfulness to the most common listening concerns of the Information Age. These include:

- Do I have attention deficit disorder?

- Continuing to sharpen the saw

- How to listen better in meetings or classes

- Remembering people's names

- Listening hygiene

- Skillful listening

If you have been faithful to your daily breathing practice, you probably notice an improved ability to direct and maintain your attention. One of my students, Adam, a sales manager at a software company, complained that his main problem with listening was that he was easily lured by other information sources in his environment. When listening to a customer or employee complaint, he was tempted to pick up a memo, glance at his e-mail, or answer the phone. He felt anxious about not getting enough done during the day and missing out on opportunities coming at him from all angles.

Eventually, Adam was able to see that his scattered attention and his negligence of customer and employee relationships was the true source of his anxiety. He spent so much time having to put out fires brought on by mindless inattention to people that he had nothing left over for his office work. After a few weeks of meditation practice, Adam reported that he was less fidgety and more able to resist the urge to give in to the computer and the phone. Adam discovered that he could shift his attention back to listening in the movie and solve problems more efficiently, to the satisfaction of both his customers and his employees. This gave him more free time to stay informed, read his e-mail, and return calls. He said:

> I started to see the connection after a few days of breathing prac-
> tice. Before then, when someone came in with a problem, I couldn't
> keep still enough to focus on the issue. Other things seemed so
> much more important to me. I felt scattered between the work on
> my desk and this person talking, so by the end of the day I paid
> the consequences. After I started meditating, the same distrac-
> tions didn't pull me away as easily. Now I'm able to stay with my
> breath for longer periods without other thoughts competing for
> attention. Without being hard on myself, I calmly notice these
> other thoughts and then return to my breath. That was the turn-
> ing point. Now I'm more patient and able to get into the movie of
> the person talking. Even on a people-busy day, I have more time
> left over to do my desk work.

Do I Have Attention Deficit Disorder?

Some students arrive at my listening workshops fully convinced that
their listening problems are related to attention deficit disorder, better known as ADD. Even without an official diagnosis, it is easy to
convince yourself that this is your problem. The name itself, *attention deficit disorder,* sounds precisely like what ails many of us—namely,
difficulty staying focused. ADD appears to be tailormade for our
high-tech, fast-paced culture. There are so many auditory and visual
stimuli and so little time to process them that we struggle to stay
afloat in a sea of information. Researchers at Washington State University found that in 1995, office visits made to a physician for the
treatment of ADD had doubled to 2,357,833 since 1990. Evan I.
Schwartz, writing in the June 1994 issue of *Wired* magazine, describes
ADD as "the official brain syndrome of the information age." True

adult ADD, however, can include several behaviors, ranging from mild to severe. Some of the most common include:

- Inability to maintain attention to structured tasks
- Difficulty following directions
- Sticking to deadlines
- Fidgeting, difficulty sitting still
- Excessive interrupting
- Impulsive behaviors

It should be noted that although millions of people suffer with ADD, the disorder is present in less than 5 percent of the adult population, and that a true diagnosis of ADD can be made only by an experienced physician or psychologist. ADD may be difficult to diagnose because it can be masked by other conditions—depression, obsessive-compulsive disorder, thyroid gland dysfunction, or anxiety. Also, there is no standard test that can definitively label an adult as having ADD. Currently ADD is thought to be a neurobehavioral disorder of self-control that usually starts in childhood and persists into adulthood. Although ADD is thought by some researchers to be a genetically transmitted disorder, the behavior characteristics of ADD are becoming so common (the average kindergarten through eighth-grade teacher may report five or more children correctly or incorrectly diagnosed with ADD per classroom per year) that many psychologists believe that it is culturally induced. A school nurse recently told me that she spends more and more of her day running from classroom to classroom, administering medications to children who have been labeled with this syndrome.

Information comes at us from all angles: TV, radio, the Internet, fax machines, e-mail, voice mail, and regular mail. There are so much data available to us that we have a difficult time sorting out what is relevant and important. As the public is made more aware of the symptoms of ADD, it is tempting to joke about having this disorder as an excuse for the mindless listening habits we display daily. However, an adult with true ADD experiences these behaviors *consistently*, not just a few times a day.

It is even more desirable to consider a drug as a quick solution to the problem instead of looking deep within ourselves for the answer. Our barriers, our ever-expanding must-do lists, and forgotten sense of calm actually prevent us from focusing on any one thing.

Diagnosis of adult ADD begins with a visit with your primary physician. She may suggest a consultation with a psychologist to rule out depression, anxiety, or stress-related illness. If the diagnosis is confirmed, the usual and most effective course of treatment is medication. Frequently prescribed medications for ADD include Ritalin, Cylert, Norpramin, Torfranil, Dexadrine, Prozac, and Aderall. It is wise to discuss treatment options with your physician, including any long and short-term side effects of the prescribed medication.

Remember that medication alleviates only the symptoms and side effects of ADD—what may remain are the old coping behaviors that need to be deconstructed and rebuilt. Dr. Kevin Murphy, chief of the ADD clinic at the University of Massachusetts Medical Center, reports that once a patient is relieved of the mental storm associated with ADD through the use of medication, it is still necessary to modify the habits of communicating that accompanied the old ADD behaviors. This is also true for persons clinically diagnosed with depression or anxiety disorders whose balance has been restored with the use of medication. For example, after years of Ritalin or Prozac, some old reflexive patterns may persist, such as inattention, self-absorption, impulsive speaking, and negative self-talk. In a more mentally and emotionally balanced state, thanks to medication, the person is now in a position to rekindle old relationships and take advantage of new opportunities. This is where mindful listening helps a person to

- experience a formerly unattainable state of relaxation

- widen the comfort zone for new ideas that once were threatening

- concentrate better in lectures and discussions

- put aside self-concerns to understand others

Continuing to Sharpen the Saw

It is widely accepted that a certain amount of memory loss can be attributed to biological changes associated with age. However, some percentage of memory loss may be a conditioned expectation. We may have witnessed grandparents becoming absentminded and forgetful, but we may not have been aware of other factors contributing to their memory changes, such as depression, reduced socialization, illness, or hearing loss. Very few of our grandparents' generation went on to pursue continuing education or new careers after retiring from the jobs they held for thirty or more years. Therefore, we expect memory loss to creep in and perhaps allow ourselves to become lazy when listening. My neighbor, a gentleman in his late seventies, told me about his memory loss.

> After all, people my age are all slowing down a bit and changing physically. Why should we hold ourselves to younger standards of mental sharpness? Nobody expects us to remember everything the same way as before. Even people who don't know me see that I'm older and assume that my mind is old, too. They speak louder and talk to me like I'm a baby sometimes . . . simple sentences, to help me understand and remember, I guess.

Even though more and more people over age sixty are going back to school and starting up businesses, the majority of seniors feel due to stereotypical thinking that their capacity for new learning is diminished.

Many historical and contemporary studies of brain activity support the fact that at least five auditory-association areas of the brain participate when we listen to spoken language. Both left and right hemispheres are activated during listening tasks. The more complex tasks (i.e., listening for details, use of visualization, linking dates with events requiring silent rehearsal) involve even more brain activity.

As the amount of auditory stimuli increases, we run the risk of listening on autopilot—skimming the surface for information that falls into the category of our self-interests or supports our biases. Analysis and comparison take too much time and threaten the status quo. After all, it's much more convenient to just skip over what doesn't fit . . . or is it?

Long-term memory (LTM) (also called *semantic* memory) is the filter that chooses what information to save for short-term storage, awareness, and long-term storage. LTM determines what is relevant and worth capturing and what can be discarded. It is an efficient way to manage massive amounts of information. Anxiety can thwart the process, either as a result of too much information assailing the system at once or as an ever-present condition that blocks all data needed to make a decision or take appropriate action. The source of the anxiety that affects our ability to listen mindfully is often related to the barriers discussed in chapter four.

In normal activity, millions of brain cells die every day. Research shows that when our brains are active, we retain more brain cells and are able to sprout new ones. Listening invigorates the brain. Positron emission tomography (PET) scans show that blood flow increases to many parts of the brain during listening. As we age, our lives become more routine and predictable, but this approach offers little opportunity to expand our repertoire for new knowledge and new ways of thinking. There is evidence that we can slow down the inevitable aging process of the brain by simply putting our brains to work *more* every day rather than less.

Many of us can boast acquaintance with an elderly person whom we describe as "sharp as a tack." Through *accelerated* brain use versus *stagnant* brain use, these individuals defy the connection between old age and senility. It is still possible to develop Alzheimer's or a similar dementia if it runs in your family, despite attempts to actively use the brain. However, the majority of us can prevent or postpone dysfunctional memory loss by continually sharpening the saw every day through mindful listening.

In my workshops, I like to shock my audience with the benefits of mindful listening. In one exercise, I tell them that they will be listening to a five-minute commentary from a radio talk show. Half of the group is instructed to listen for the name of the speaker, her background, her main argument, as least two points that support it, and to tell how the speaker felt about the issue. The second half of the group is asked to just listen.

Each group is unaware of the instructions given to the other. Without fail, at least 90 percent of the group that was given specific instructions are able to recall considerably more information than the group that was told to "just listen." A short quiz hours later at the end of the workshop reveals that the mindful-listening group still retains at least 75 percent of the commentary. If you want to retain the information, it makes sense to embark on a listening opportunity with certain goals in mind:

- Get to know the speaker's name and background. What life experiences led him to these conclusions?

- What is his main point? What facts or observations support his position?

- How does he feel about the topic?

- How does his point of view add or change your view of the issue?

Depending on the nature of the conversation, you may want to listen with more or less structure. For example, if your customer is telling you about her new job or your child is complaining about too much homework, your only concern might be to learn how the person *feels* about her situation. The degree of vigilance you employ depends on the extent of the information the speaker is willing to share and how much you want or need to remember.

From a listening perspective alone, your ability to focus, select, and process auditory information bombarding the airwaves every day is a daunting task. If you haven't tried this recently, notice how difficult it is to process two speakers simultaneously. You begin to follow speaker A's message, and as you shift your attention to speaker B, notice how speaker A might as well be speaking a foreign language. You may be able to process some of the gestural and vocal cues of speaker A, but not the verbal message. This shows that you can really listen to only one thing at a time.

To remember better, you need regular practice at being absorbed with the speaker and what he has to say by getting into his movie or listening in a mindful way. This gives you the chance to involve both sides of the brain—the left side, which processes the logical meanings of words, and the right side, which takes the speaker's tone and nonverbal gestures into account.

Hence, when you are totally absorbed, your brain is actively engaged on many levels over a period of minutes. Compare that level of mental aerobics with the typical listener's attention span. With regular application of breathing meditation and the movie mindset, you can shift into gear and stay there throughout an interaction.

Get practice staying in the movie in noisy places. Even if familiar people walk by as you listen to your speaker, resist the urge to nod or wave. Nothing else matters but the person you are listening to. With this kind of practice, just think how much easier it will be to focus your listening in quieter environments.

If you continually challenge your listening capacity, you will be exercising more of your brain. Most of us use only 7 to 8 percent of our brain power daily. Dr. Patrick Turski, of the University of Wisconsin Hospital, has patients listen to Charlton Heston reading passages by Nietzsche. This is done for the purpose of mapping areas of the brain involved in verbal processing. In 1997, during a surgical procedure to remove a congenital malformation from the brain of a thirty-one-year-old woman, it was essential to locate these sites of speech and language processing prior to the actual surgery in order to avoid brain damage. Nietzsche was chosen because, according to Dr. Turski, complicated philosophical literature encourages more brain activity and concentration, and requires the listener to utilize higher orders of verbal processing. Not only are the primary listening centers activated, but also the association areas of the brain. Compare the complexity of a philosophical discussion with the complexity of the average sitcom. Given the fact that many of us spend more time watching TV than engaging in intellectual discussions, is it any wonder that our attention and concentration skills are dwindling?

How else might we exercise our brains? Radio talk shows, books on tape, and continuing education courses are low-cost ways to improve attention and comprehension. Paraphrase the speaker's ideas back to yourself aloud. This allows you to clarify new ideas and store them in your memory bank.

To improve your ability to process and recall factual or technical information, take ten to twenty minutes every day to listen to a radio interview, self-help tape, or lecture. At the midpoint and at the end of the segment *say back aloud* some of the key points you heard. Elaborate on one or two of them, if possible. Just like in the paraphrasing exercise in chapter five, unless you can paraphrase the key points out loud to yourself, you will not know whether you have processed the information. With practice, this daily exercise can considerably increase your confidence in your memory! Experts in memory agree—*use it or lose it.*

Commercials can be helpful in giving us that minute of recall opportunity. After listening to a portion of a TV or radio interview, for example, use the commercial time to recall issues and key points. Review aloud so you can hear the completeness of your ideas. If the material is of particular interest, go one step further and jot down these ideas on paper. Occasional review of the material helps keep the information accessible for future use. You'll be surprised to see that later that day, you will be able to relate to others several points on that particular issue.

Another way to improve your ability to concentrate, particularly when the information is technical or complex, is to *picture the words* as they are being spoken, like a teletype in your mind's eye. This definitely takes practice, but it can be very helpful in a dry lecture or a technical explanation. Some of us learn better when information is presented visually, while some of us learn even better when information is presented visually *and* aurally. An advantage to this method is that it eliminates external distractions because you are so busy listening *and* seeing in your mind's eye every word that is being uttered.

Many people feel that taking notes should be reserved for the classroom, or that it is a sign of poor memory to take out a notepad and jot down a few points. Most speakers would agree, however, that any sign of conscientious listening is appreciated. At least you can be sure that the message was received. In addition, writing down and seeing the information in print, even if you discard the notes shortly afterward, means that there will be a better chance of recall at a later date.

Once you choose to remember some piece of information, dwell on it for *at least one minute*. This allows the association areas of your brain to get in on the act and take that piece of information to a deeper level. Douglas J. Herrman, the author of *Super Memory*, claims that anything given less than a minute of thought will fade from memory. Once the words are perceived and you choose to remember the idea, it takes several seconds of rehearsal or repetition of the information to make it to short-term memory. For example, when you have to remember a phone number, you usually repeat it several times before you call. Yet by the time the call is complete, you may have forgotten it again. Occasional rehearsal of your new association keeps the information in long-term storage. (For specific help with memory, please see the bibliography at the back of this book.)

Dr. Tony Buzan introduced an effective means of note making/taking called *mind mapping*. This technique is contrary to the standard system of writing out full sentences or making an outline. Dr. Buzan states that the traditional style of note taking uses *less than half* of the capacity of the brain to learn new information. In fact, traditional note taking works against the brain's natural inclination to learn by making associations and looking for patterns. Traditional note taking obscures key ideas, is monotonous, uses listening time inefficiently, and fails to stimulate the brain to remember. Consequently, we diminish our powers of concentration, view learning as time consuming and unproductive, lose confidence in our ability to learn, and because we are working against the brain's natural tendencies, we become frustrated with learning. In contrast, mind mapping incorporates images and pictures with printed words. Ideas hover around a central theme. Various modes of print and the use of spacing and symmetrical designs help the brain remember ideas associated with the central theme.

You may ask, what is Zen-like about mind mapping? Mind

mapping doesn't restrict us to just the words of the message. Our map can include emphases, contrasts, feelings, and complexity unlike a flat list of words and phrases. Mind mapping is liberating. It frees the brain from barriers to learning—monotony, frustration, and poor self-esteem. It is also a mindful activity because it promotes concentration and creativity.

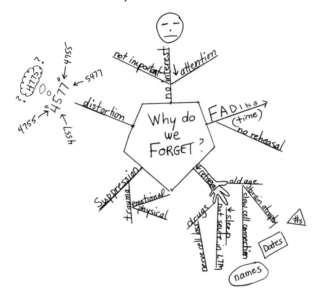

How to Listen Better in Meetings and Classes

If you do not give your full attention to the speaker, the information will not have a chance to get into your memory. Students frequently ask how to maintain attention during large meetings, particularly the boring ones. CNN recently claimed that at least 38 percent of people polled have difficulty paying attention in meetings.

Why are certain meetings more boring than others? A poll taken from thirty students chosen at random from my classes revealed the following. When asked to fill in the blank: "A meeting is considered

boring or a waste of time because it _____."
Most students completed the sentence in one of four ways: 1) "will require no input from me or the people in my group," 2) "lacks an agenda, or does not stick to the proposed agenda," 3) "accomplishes nothing," 4) "is led by a poor speaker."

Students also feel resentment that they are forced to listen in these situations, and subsequently, find it difficult to tune back in when necessary. In the next chapter, you will see how you as a meeting presenter can keep the number of poor listeners to a minimum. But for now, as potentially gifted listeners, how can you become mindful in meetings and get the most out of them?

Just calling a meeting or a presentation "boring" implies that it has no purpose and that it is a waste of time. But if you tweak your attitude toward these kinds of activities and approach meetings as an archeological dig or a challenge to discover an idea you may not have otherwise encountered, you will benefit. Some of the great entrepreneurs of our time say that great ideas come to them in unexpected situations. A word or phrase triggers a series of associations that leads to a new invention or a solution to a problem. Use you ears' *downtime* (the lag between the mind's ability to process information and the speaker's rate of speech) to review what has been said and its relevance to current trends, articles you've read, or implications for future endeavors. Remember that your focus, although broadened by the associations you are making, is still in the present with the speaker in the foreground. Find out how this piece, this topic, is part of the big picture.

For example, I was required to attend a manager's meeting at our clinic about the employee parking problem, a topic that might be considered well within the definition of boring. Instead of taking that attitude, I sat back and was astounded to hear a wide variety of solutions. Some were practical, others convenient but costly, several were creative. One person presented an ethical approach. By combining a few of these ideas, we were able to strike a majority vote and arrive at a remedy. If I had given myself twenty minutes to come up with all the possible solutions to the parking problem, I would have thought of only a couple at best. Listening with barriers down to these diverse perspectives widened my scope for solving my own business problems that day.

If a more active approach is necessary, take a bold step by offering to take the minutes of the meeting. This requires you to be totally focused. Firsthand experience taught me the value of getting involved in this way, even when I assumed that the meeting had little to do with me. Given the task to take the minutes (the secretary was out sick), others depended on me to become absorbed in the issues discussed. As I took notes, I realized that the ideas being proposed would help a coworker who was having problems with one of her projects. I became invested in the concerns of the group. By the end of the meeting, not only was I able to provide the team leader with an accurate and detailed report, but I had picked up some tips for my friend and learned quite a bit for myself.

The usual mindset would have set me apart, twiddling my thumbs and watching the clock in boredom. I also felt guilty, thinking of other meetings in the past that I had classified as boring—what lost opportunities! Students in my listening classes admit that at first, they are reluctant to take the minutes because they doubt their ability to catch everything; they have been such passive participants for so long. But with practice, the rewards are immediate, and they jump at the chance to give the secretary a break!

Taking the minutes, like other listening exercises described in this book, is a daunting task for some—it challenges our barriers and concentration skills. But these are the missions for the mind that wait at your doorstep every day.

Remembering People's Names

We love it when someone remembers our name. It makes us feel good about our uniqueness, the impression we made, or the possibility of a future relationship. When someone says they remember our face but (sorry!) not our name, we are not as enthusiastic.

Forgetting names is one of the most common communication complaints, but it is fairly easy to remedy with practice and the proper mindset. Comedian Paul Rieser had a great solution to this dilemma. He suggested we eliminate names altogether and refer to each other according to our unique physical characteristics. Instead of saying "Hey Jim, meet Mary," we could say "Hey, Broken Glasses, come on over here and meet Food in Her Teeth!" In a way, this approach has merit.

Think about the names you are able to recall and ask yourself why that is. Of course we remember the names of family members, but can you explain why you remember Harold, a brief acquaintance from twelve years ago? Is it that you recall the coincidence of going to the movie *Harold and Maude* and joking about his choice in movies? Or was it that he was the "spittin' image" of your Uncle Harold? Nevertheless, the names of people that you spent much more time with twelve years ago may elude you. Chances are, it was the association of the name with something already familiar that set Harold's name in stone.

Try this: every time you meet someone new, associate a prominent characteristic with his name. For instance, someone named Jim may be very slender, so it's handy to think of him as "Slim Jim." The next time you run into Jim, his outstanding feature—his slimness—will pop into your mind and "Jim" will surface. Or you may recall a Jim in your past who looks very much like *this* Jim.

My favorite method of remembering names is to repeat the name during the handshake and a few times during our conversation. This means: 1) at the introduction, 2) when initiating a comment, and 3) at the close of the discussion. People love to hear their names, but don't overdo it. During this time you are in their movie and assimilating information about them with their name solidly in the mix. Repeating a person's name throughout the conversation assists you in making the connections needed for recall later on. When your intention is to develop a working relationship with that person, your occasional repetition of his name will feel more natural. If, on the other hand, you treat a new acquaintance as a meal ticket, your use of his name will come across as phony.

As extra insurance, soon after the discussion, write down the name and any notes about a new acquaintance. Review the information occasionally, rehearse the association, particularly when you might run into your new acquaintance again. Rehearsal (seeing the person's face and what was discussed while repeating the name) is particularly helpful with unusual names.

As our society becomes more culturally diverse, we encounter more and more unfamiliar names. This renders the association approach practically useless. In my clinic, I frequently come across physicians and nurses from other countries. Names like Fanghua, Sangbaek and Thanatip are difficult to pronounce correctly, much less remember. These foreign-born associates already feel isolated by the language barrier and cultural differences, and this may be exacerbated by American-born colleagues who are hesitant to initiate conversation for fear of mispronouncing their names. We welcome the nicknames that are more familiar to us, like Bob, Mike, or Liz, yet we cannot expect foreign-born people to change their names just for our convenience.

Most people heartily appreciate being addressed by name. When I teach foreign-accent reduction classes, I see it as a personal challenge and a necessity to learn twenty or more students' names within a week. Establishing this link sets the stage for openness and self-discovery. The first step is to be sure to pronounce each name correctly. When you meet someone with an unusual name, *insist* upon getting the pronunciation correct. The spelling might not help, so grab a piece of paper and write out phonetically, as closely as possible, the right pronunciation. Getting comfortable with the pronunciation is a necessary first step, and I have yet to meet a foreign-born person who is not willing to persist with me until I get it right. Then I repeat the name a few times during our conversation. Shortly thereafter, I recall the conversation and the name. This takes consistent practice, but the rewards will encourage you to make it a habit.

By the way, if you do forget someone's name, ask it again and give this process another try. Otherwise, you know how it goes—you'll be playing the search-my-brain-for-the-name game while completely tuning out what he is saying. My students are at first reluctant to accept that the forgotten other will not be upset with them. On the contrary, he or she whose name you forgot sees your request as admirable (admitting the mind-slip up front) and confident (taking action to get it right the second time). It also lets them know you care enough to admit your flaw.

A very considerate gesture when running into people you know only marginally is to immediately reintroduce yourself. They will be very grateful to you for the minirefresher, and both of you can concentrate on your message rather than playing the name game while you speak.

Using the person's name during the conversation may feel odd at first, but with a couple of tries, it will start to feel natural. We are used to trying to relate to someone while standing outside the theater. With the names attached to the movie, you can both get down to knowing one another.

Listening Hygiene

From a physical point of view, there are things you can do to improve your ability to listen. First, ask yourself a few questions:

Do you get enough sleep? If your mind is not awake and alert, how can you be a mindful listener? Most of us need at least seven to eight hours of sleep a night in order to attend and concentrate efficiently. According to James Maas, the author of *Power Sleep,* we may find ourselves falling asleep during meetings, not because of the content, the room temperature, or the heavy lunch we just consumed, but because these conditions expose the level of sleep deprivation in our bodies. Because our consciousness during sleep doesn't appear to have the same continuity and focus as waking consciousness, most people think that when we are asleep the brain is turned off. Quite the contrary. For example, REM (rapid eye movement) sleep, the state of sleep associated with dreaming, is known as *paradoxical sleep* because, despite the relaxed tone of the body, the brain and respiratory system are very active. REM sleep stimulates neural circuits that retain ideas and memories. Without strong memory circuits acquired during REM sleep, we may have difficulty remembering what we hear over the course of a day.

How do you fuel the fire for listening? Sometimes our most important meetings of the day occur right after lunch. Rather than listening to the message, our bodies are preoccupied with digesting. Overeating can lead to drowsiness, which impairs our ability to pay attention. On the other hand, being hungry and drinking too much caffeine can make us jumpy and easily distractible. Some people feel that they are better communicators after a few alcoholic drinks. They report being more relaxed, less inhibited. Unfortunately, *accurate* processing of the message is poorer under the influence of alcohol, and after a few drinks it may be difficult to stay awake. Over time, the effects of alcohol have been found to seriously impair memory.

Gingko supplements, used with caution (gingko should not be taken with certain heart medications), have been advertised as memory enhancers. However, there appear to be no well-controlled studies to support this claim yet.

In order to maximize your readiness to listen, get to know the amounts and kinds of foods that best enable your brain to perform at its best. To exceed that threshold spells disaster for attention and concentration.

Are you anxious or depressed? Anxiety and depression make it difficult to get into the movie or to be mindful. Our barriers (described in chapter four) cause major distractions, or you may be preoccupied with internal struggles, as discussed in chapter five. Your ability to listen mindfully may also be affected by physical tension, which, as I have stated throughout this book, can be mitigated significantly through meditation.

When was your last yearly physical examination? Physiological imbalances can cause difficulties with memory. We already discussed the effects of alcohol and caffeine, but certain medications may also affect your ability to process and recall information.

Hormonal imbalances have also been cited as responsible for memory loss and learning difficulties. Women who are estrogen deficient may also suffer from cognitive disorders. According to a study in the *Journal of the American Medical Association,* "Effects of Age, Sex, and Ethnicity on the Association Between Apolipoprotein E Genotype and Alzheimer Disease: A Meta-analysis" (Vol. 278, No. 16), women are also two to three times more likely to develop Alzheimer's disease than men. Dr. Roberta Diaz Brinton at the University of Southern California claims that "some, not all, estrogens will promote the cellular mechanism responsible for learning and memory and protect them from the damage that occurs from free radicals and some of the insults that are associated with Alzheimer's disease." Diabetics should also consult their physicians if memory problems are noted.

Skillful Listening

Mindful listening provides the basis for skillful listening, or decision-based mindful listening. Some of you may be familiar with the term *critical listening*. In our information-laden world, we simply do not have the time to listen to everything that comes our way, so we have to make decisions between listening to things we *should* hear and what we *want* to hear. There are approximately eighteen hundred radio talk shows in America. When one comes on about how to reduce your risk of heart disease, it is quite tempting to see what the fight is about on the Jerry Springer show. Sometimes we merely want to be entertained by watching unusual people do unusual things, or we may be just plain curious about the motives of a mass murderer. We must ask ourselves, "Will this show benefit me in some way? Or will it add more noise or bolster a barrier I've been trying to get rid of?"

It is necessary to seriously examine the quality and integrity of the discussions, advertisements, and news reports that influence what car to buy, what candidate to vote for, what vitamins to take, how much coffee to drink, what stocks to buy, and how much exercise we need. Because of our limited attention spans, we are drawn to the more sensational speakers and advertisements and tempted to tune out the lengthy, less attractive presenters that may be the most informative.

As mindful listeners, we take an objective stance in listening for the truth. We are aware of the methods used by the media to persuade and sell. For example, an advertising agency discovered that despite our years of quality education our attention span is about twenty-two seconds. Ah! Just about as long as the average commercial! Nowadays, infomercials push our limits to fifteen minutes or more. They frequently feature fast-talking, enthusiastic, handsome celebrities who repeat over and over again the benefits of the product.

But as mindful listeners, we know how our eyes frequently take precedence over our ears. Lesley Stahl, a reporter on the television show *60 Minutes,* describes in *Reporting Live* how television overpowers our reason. She cites a news report she prepared on the theme of how President Reagan used television to create an image of himself that was contrary to his actual stand on issues such as funding for the disabled and housing for the elderly. In support of her thesis, Stahl used footage of Reagan presiding at the opening of a nursing home and presenting medals to Special Olympics athletes. Despite her voice-over describing Reagan's actual position on these issues, the Reagan White House was overjoyed with her reportage. They insisted that Stahl's critical voice-over had made no impact on the viewing audience, that only the video portion of her report was important. A short time later, Stahl's piece was shown without the sound track to an audience of 100 people. When they were asked what the report was about, they claimed it was a political promo. The clip was replayed, this time with Stahl's critical audio commentary. Still, over half the audience insisted it was a very pro-Reagan news report!

Stahl says, "Unlike reading or listening to the radio, with television we 'learn' with two of our senses together, and apparently the eye is dominant. . . . We get an emotional reaction: the information doesn't always go to the thinking part of our brains but to the gut." As voters and consumers, we need to be aware of this tendency to perceive information in an unbalanced way. By strengthening our listening abilities, we become more competent decision makers.

Here are some questions you might ask yourself while listening to TV or radio: What are the pros and cons in what the speaker proposes? Skillful listening means making associations with what the speaker is promoting and what you know from prior knowledge or experience. Aside from just getting the facts, is her argument well supported? If not, why? Is she an expert in her field? What are the short and long-term implications of what this person is suggesting? What is her bias?

Pharmaceutical companies are well aware of our listening weaknesses, particularly of the less medically educated market. A fast-growing segment of the population spends billions of dollars on health and beauty products directed toward promoting longevity and youthfulness. Even if you purchase only vitamin C tablets every few months, you are a target for the industry. It is tempting to think that a pill can improve your memory or give you more energy. After all, pills are effective for losing weight, eliminating depression, and keeping you awake. Why not trust a pill that will make you smarter?

The companies selling herbal remedies must include credible sources in their commercials, just like advertisers of aspirin and antacids. At best, they may have a few satisfied customers (or people paid to act like satisfied customers) and an endorsement by a believable person. Is that enough to convince you to spend twenty dollars or more on a pill? Sometimes. But to make sure, these companies often cite a research study claiming positive findings. What the average listener does not hear is whether the studies performed included a sizeable and representative population, were well controlled for accuracy, or overseen by a reputable association like a major clinic or scientific organization.

In addition, it is difficult—or perhaps impossible—to quantify an intangible benefit like energy or memory. Feeling younger and smarter is in the eye of the beholder. The unskillful listener will slap down cash not knowing what to expect and without hearing any hard evidence to support the claims. Health product advertising is only one venue that requires skillful listening.

How well are *you* prepared for listening in the twenty-first century? Developing your foundation of mindful listening will ready you for the onslaught of information, advertising, diversity, and hype predicted in this millennium.

Ask yourself

- Are you a fair listener?

- Is your listening focused and concentrated in order to use the knowledge base you have acquired to examine the validity of the evidence?

- Can you process information contrary to your beliefs with out becoming defensive or argumentative?

- Can you look beyond physical attractiveness and sensational claims to evaluate the validity of the product or service?

- Is your negative self-talk under control or do you mistrust your gut feeling?

Cortical Calisthenics

1. Prior to a listening opportunity like a TV or radio interview, review the list of questions above. Discuss your answers with a friend who also saw or heard the same show. Agree with a partner to regularly practice mindful listening in this manner.

2. Sign up for an adult education class. Most large towns or cities have at least one adult education program. Some colleges and universities offer adult education programs also. These affordable classes can run anywhere from two to eight hours on a single day to two to four hours once every six weeks, depending upon the format. You can take in a minilecture or learn a new skill.

3. When you go to view an exhibit at an art museum, spend a few extra dollars and take the tour on tape. These audio guide programs can be very entertaining and will enhance your appreciation and understanding of the work by narrating the history surrounding the piece, the artist's mood, or events that shaped the work.

How to Help Others Listen Better

It is no use walking anywhere to preach
unless our walking is our preaching.

—Saint Francis of Assisi

Why aren't we taught listening skills in school? Given the fact that it is the basis for learning math, science, and reading, not to mention many other life skills, you would think that listening classes would occupy a prominent position in the academic curriculum. Browse through your local library and you will find dozens of books on how to write or how to be a better public speaker, but you will find very few books on listening—the nation's greatest communication weakness.

As we mature into adulthood, listening acquires several negative connotations. For instance, when someone says, "Listen to me," we interpret that as "Agree with me," or "Do as I say," thus relinquishing control and taking a back seat to the speaker. Isn't it ironic that the number-one request of teachers is to "pay attention"? When I was a kid, that was code for, "Look up you heathens, stop doing what you're enjoying and suffer while I talk."

These unpleasant associations give listening a bad rap. By the time we are adults, we view listening as passive and speaking as a leadership activity. Rarely in commercials are political candidates shown listening. Because listening is an internal, silent process, it lacks the visual flashiness needed to grab voters' attention. In actual political life, however, the average politician claims to spend at least 70 percent of his job listening. Therefore, wouldn't it make sense to vote for the better listener?

In July 1999, Hillary Rodham Clinton launched her listening tours as part of her campaign for the New York Senate seat. It was a novel strategy and it made a lot of sense. First of all, the people of New York knew Mrs. Clinton better than she knew them, and she had, compared to her competition, little time to get to know voters. She chose the most direct route to developing a relationship with voters—letting them know she *wanted to listen.* When a candidate listens in mindfulness, open to dissenting opinions with an eagerness to understand, voters feel valued. If Senator Clinton brands herself as "the candidate who listens," it will be interesting to see how far this refreshing campaign approach takes her.

In American schools, about twelve years of formal education are focused on teaching us how to read, write, and speak. Yet according to Madelyn Burley-Allen in *Listening—the Forgotten Skill,* only about half a year, doled out in bits and pieces without any structured format, comprises listening training. Yet our ability to excel in reading, speaking, and writing depends on the strength of our listening and concentration skills. Studies show that elementary students are expected on the average to spend 57.5 percent of their classroom time listening; high-school students 66 percent; and college students, anywhere from 52 to 90 percent.

Perhaps listening is one of those skills that teachers assume we learn at home. Those of us who were fortunate enough to have frequent family discussions practiced turn-taking, debate, and critical listening from an early age. This preliminary coaching prepared us for learning how to reason, analyze information (spoken or written), and the give and take required in making friends.

Even dogs need some basic training from their mothers before they can be adopted by humans. Prior to bringing home my beloved Spud from the litter next door, I read a book called *Mother Knows Best.* It explained how mother dogs instinctively discipline their pups to take turns feeding, to be submissive, to clean themselves, and protect their food. The mother sets up certain conditions, and it's up to the human owner to follow through immediately with the next stages of training.

The lack of preschool home training makes classroom learning difficult for so many children. If basic attention and listening skills were emphasized in the home from an early age, teachers would be able to use their talents to teach instead of having to constantly discipline children who have never been prepared to learn. More time spent on teaching would probably result in better SAT scores and more fulfilled adults. I propose that daily discussions about everyday moral dilemmas, vacation planning, household chores, sports, and so on, be standard topics at the dinner table, on automobile trips, and during bedtime conversation.

Signing our children up for a listening class may not be the best way for them to become better listeners, especially if it is not given the same credibility as science or math. Children learn best by observing and imitating their parents. Be a good model of listening not only in the home environment, but also in social situations. Show your children how disputes and differences of opinion can be tolerated and, in some cases, even welcomed.

Teach your children at an early age that a different way of doing things does not have to be accompanied by a judgment. When you watch a movie together or see a different mode of dress, avoid judgmental remarks. Balance the negative aspects of any experience with positive observations. Allow for some gray areas before a final decision is made. Pick out routine activities and demonstrate different ways of achieving the same solution. For example, when driving to a familiar destination, choose a different route and notice your child's reaction. Reassure her that there may be some delight in taking a slightly longer route once in awhile. Or take your kids to an ethnic restaurant. To increase the chances of your child appreciating this break from the cherished pizza-and-burger routine, ask the waiter which foods on the menu are particularly favored by children their age. They still may not like the cuisine, but you can emphasize that this is a chance to see how kids in other lands eat every day. A new experience does not always have to be a favorite one in order to be beneficial.

Kids learn how to listen by being listened to. And just like adults, kids want to share those good feelings by listening to others. In my listening utopia I envision families sitting down to meditate together for ten to fifteen minutes every morning before work or play. This would settle down mental distractions and fine tune their abilities to absorb the contents of the day. More attention would be paid to calm discussion instead of mindless TV and radio. As the result of good listening, parents and teachers would receive respect and loyalty, the difficult people in our lives would receive compassion, and the thoughts and perspectives of people from other cultures would be welcomed.

Another awakening experience occurred to me during my work as a voice coach. Managers thrust into the world of public speaking, salespeople, and budding political candidates made up my "Enhancing Your Vocal Image" classes. The main theme of the class was "It's not *what* you say but *how* you say it." This class became increasingly popular as media experts shared their insights about political candidates, particularly around election time. We heard commentators hail Ronald Reagan as "the great communicator," not because of how he listened or chose his words, but because of his charismatic voice and commanding presence. He also had an excellent speechwriter. George Bush presented a striking contrast. His weak, whiny voice and agitated responses under stress earned him a reputation as a wimp. The eighties taught us much about the image makers in politics and big business, and how we could get ahead using some of their techniques.

My voice-image class focused on creating a physical presence on stage, using techniques borrowed from actors' workshops and the professional image makers to wow the audience or win the sale. Many students claimed that these methods earned them the vote, the sale, the promotion, despite the fact that the presentation was often badly prepared or the sales pitch failed to make sense.

Those admissions, despite the students' delight at beating out the competition, gave me a queasy feeling. I began to rethink the purpose of passing down these gems of knowledge and experience from my days in theater. Not long after that revelation, I had an opportunity that forever changed my way of communication training.

In 1992, I was invited to visit Senator Paul Tsongas and convince him to improve his vocal image. He was a presidential candidate for the Democrat Party, and although he was well respected for his knowledge and integrity, he was handicapped by voice characteristics and a presentation style that lacked the power and punch expected of the leader of the most powerful country on Earth. Senator Tsongas listened patiently to my dissertation on what I could do to improve his speaking style. A few supporters who were also present urged him to consider the coaching. Soon after our meeting, however, I received word that Senator Tsongas chose not to follow through with voice coaching. Despite his desire for victory and the knowledge that his lackluster speaking style could cost him the nomination, Senator Tsongas could not bring himself to sound different to his wife and children. What I judged as a small concession for a big prize, Senator Tsongas saw as a threat to what mattered to him most—his honesty with himself and others.

From that point on, I continued to teach the same skills, but with the motive of helping others to listen better and understand the message rather than swaying an audience to act in our self-interest.

To help others listen when we speak involves:

- connecting with your listeners, making it easy for them to get into your movie;

- forming a trusting relationship with them (how many products you sell when your presentation is over, getting your kids to clear off the dinner dishes, or getting your husband to mow the lawn are secondary);

- being mindful about what your audience wants and needs to know;

- knowing their barriers toward you.

If you want others to listen and understand you better, think about what makes *you* want to listen. High on your list may be compliments, words of encouragement, expressions of support, appreciation, and love, unambiguous comments and questions, or invitations to do things we like. It's easy to give orders, make demands, and criticize for the sake of getting things done, but how often do you offer an appreciative comment, compliment, or praise?

For example, my husband and I love to eat out occasionally at little ethnic restaurants, where we typically discuss our projects, family issues, or home improvements. I often think about how great it is to be with someone who enjoys these evenings too, but I couldn't remember the last time I had told him that. The next time we went out, I waited for the right moment, reached across the table and squeezed my husband's hand as I explained to him how much our evenings out meant to me. My husband smiled warmly with a glow of mutual agreement and said it made him very happy to hear that. For the rest of the evening, my husband's attentiveness to me, even with topics that would have normally stretched his interest, was spectacular.

Every parent and spouse knows the frustration of being tuned out by a loved one. As external distractions mount in our environment, being tuned out is more common than being tuned in. If you ask teenagers (specialists in this field) to tell you why they are reluctant to respond when spoken to, they will give you several reasons:

- I know what's coming . . . the dishes or something.

- It's usually homework related or something I screwed up.

- My dad always has *suggestions* for how I could do some job better next time.

- It's never anything I'm interested in hearing.

- I can't tell whether it's my mom talking or the TV—they kinda sound the same.

The message here is that teens don't see their parents' interests as relevant or interesting. Kids start building barriers toward messages with punitive overtones—like advice—at a young age. This tendency persists into adulthood and is the cause of many an unnecessary hearing test and divorce.

If by now you've discovered the joys of forgetting yourself to go to the movies, you may find it easier to let your family member finish watching the game on TV or logging off the computer before you begin talking. As I have already mentioned, meditation practice can increase the generosity of your spirit. Even though what you have to say is important, you find yourself respecting what others find more important at the time.

By letting someone finish something that is important to him, you show that he is valued and respected. That is the first step in getting someone to listen to you. Then when you are engrossed in a movie or a book and others want to interrupt, they will be more likely to show you the same courtesy. In this way, when you really need to be heard immediately, you'll have a much better chance of getting their attention.

Getting kids to listen is fraught with frustration unless you think from a mindful-listening point of view. We can become pariahs to our kids if we persist in speaking to them from our perspective. It often amuses me that the typical comments or questions, despite their inefficiency, get passed down from generation to generation. Every day we hear young parents in their twenties and thirties saying exactly the same things we grew up hearing: "Now, if you do that one more time . . ." or "Look at me! What did I just finish saying?" And how about "Wouldn't it be a nice change if we turned down the TV so I can hear myself think?" And don't forget the infamous "How many times do I have to tell you . . . ?"

After observing kids and parents interact in this manner, I doubt if the kids comprehend these threats and demands. They infer from tone of voice and body language that they're in trouble, but they don't have a clue what their parents really want. The most effective caregivers I have observed, those who succeed in keeping their kids tuned in, are the ones who say exactly what is on their minds in a nonthreatening but cooperative tone, explaining why their actions are necessary and using words kids understand: "Let's clean out the garage together today," or "Please turn down the TV. I can't hear what your father is saying."

Being flexible enough to offer choices (if choices are available) gives teenagers some say in a situation. "Your room needs to be cleaned tonight. You choose—right after dinner or before you go to bed?" Kids and adults become engrossed in external distractions like TV,

CD headphones, and the Internet. Therefore, instead of repeating yourself louder and louder, get physically closer, in full view of your listener, and speak in a normal tone. To get someone's undivided attention, try saying, "What I have to say to you right now is very important, so I need you to listen for the next ten minutes or so," or "I have something that concerns me very much that I need your opinion about," or "I know you'd rather listen to music right now, but what I have to say concerns both of us." Asking for their opinion and their assistance, using the word *important* with care, and appreciating what they are engrossed in will save you many minutes of mindless aggravation.

Perhaps your job or community requires that you give spoken presentations, or perhaps you supervise or train people at work. Getting adults to listen to you and take desirable action can be almost as challenging as getting your kids to do their homework. Adults are exposed to the same distractions as kids, and our internal distractions are greater.

Think about some of the most effective public speakers you have heard in the past.

Chances are, the ones who made the best impressions were those who did not speak *at* you but *to* you; they were sensitive to audience perspective, showed enthusiasm, and left you with a good feeling. Memorable speakers are *genuine* communicators. They care about forging a relationship with their audience. Here are sixteen ways to connect better with your audience and help them listen more effectively to the information you have to share:

1. **Get to know your audience.** Before preparing a talk for a large group, gather some information about your audience. In an impromptu situation or in a one-to-one meeting, I first get into their movie by getting them to talk so I can save time and focus my pre-

sentation on *their* best interest. This time also gives me valuable insight into their barriers. I will be able to set the stage for a better relationship if I know how they like to receive information, if they already have a bias about the topic, or if they feel uncomfortable talking to me.

2. **Keep your environment free of noise and visual distractions.** Make arrangements ahead of time for a quiet room. If you are making a presentation in an auditorium, check the microphone and adjust the lighting. Are your audiovisual aids in good working order, set appropriately, and ready to go? Ask if there are personal FM listening devices available to hearing-impaired participants. Avoid the use of distracting physical mannerisms—repetitive hand gestures, flicking back your hair, or playing with a pen or piece of jewelry.

3. **Listen first.** In gripe sessions, start by listening mindfully. When it is your turn, your speakers will be more likely to listen to you. It is so rare to come across a good listener that when we do, we feel indebted to listen to them in return. Make sure they have said everything on their minds before you begin. Allow plenty of silence between their thoughts. Until they have stopped talking, they are not ready to hear you anyway. If time is at a premium, let the audience know early on that you want to hear from as many people as possible. This will help keep each speaker to a time limit. Be flexible with your response styles.

4. **Use a bit of humor to open a presentation.** Start off with a statement that gets their attention. Comedy writer Gene Perret once said, "Humor is not a condiment; it's not a main course. It's not a trinket. It doesn't need justification; it's essential." Humor does many things to encourage listening. First, it is relaxing, and they must be relaxed in order to listen. Joking about universal human faults and

frustrations reduces tension and often makes a point better than a thousand words. Humor is entertaining and adds needed sparkle to a dry subject. Humor also helps connect you with your audience by establishing rapport. Test your jokes and stories on others before you tell an audience. Be sensitive to words that could be taken the wrong way—*girl* versus *woman,* for example. If your joke is in bad taste or poorly executed, it will have the opposite effect—it can make your audience tune you out!

5. **Use audiovisuals as supplements to highlight key ideas.** Audiences appreciate colorful slides or laptop presentations. Contact a Toastmasters club or adult education program in your community for a course in laptop presentations or listener-enhancing slide presentations.

6. **Draw diagrams to help your audience understand difficult concepts.** When speaking one-on-one or to a small group, a diagram or mind map is a great note-taking aid, often worth many words. Diagramming a simple flow chart while you speak will be retained better than a string of sentences. This approach allows more listening time and less note taking. If you are going to meet with someone whom you know in advance is not a good listener, offer her paper and pen to take notes.

7. **Emphasize key phrases by changing the pitch and pace of your words.** The use of a pause before or after a key phrase also helps to break up the hypnotic monotony of continuous talk. Research shows that a speaking rate of 275 to 300 words per minute is most conducive to listener comprehension. (See the exercises at the end of this chapter to check your speaking rate.)

8. Encourage the audience to use their visual memory. Use visually descriptive words to make a point. For example, if you are proposing a new public library in your community, you might say, "Imagine the lack of information as a dry, barren wasteland devoid of resources. Build a library and watch the land bloom green and fruitful."

9. Ask frequently for feedback from your audience. If you know their names, use them. When someone asks a question, do not assume that the whole audience heard it. Keep everyone involved by repeating the question. This also clarifies the question and helps you target your answer. After answering, inquire, "Does that answer your question?"

10. Stir up attention by breaking into a discussion format. An audience is typically more engaged when an active discussion is taking place. If you are giving a lecture and you notice that people are beginning to get that glazed look, open up the floor for discussion or debate. You may be surprised to learn that the real interests of your audience are very different from what you or your meeting planner anticipated. For example, when my dad was diagnosed with prostate cancer, I was eager to attend a lecture on the topic. The surgeon/lecturer, well known in his field, spent the first forty minutes explaining prostate anatomy and the symptoms of prostate cancer. Although this was important information, the gentleman beside me started snoring sporadically. I also sensed that many of the participants were getting restless. Finally, one bold member of the audience stood up and asked if the surgeon could discuss sex after prostate surgery, specifically his own patients' experiences. Amid the chuckles and respectful hurrahs, the surgeon smiled at his own oversight and cheerfully acquiesced. He put his notes aside, turned off the overhead projector, and got the audience involved. He did not insist on completing his agenda. Instead he unselfishly addressed the main concerns of the people who took the time to attend his lecture. He worked in some key points necessary to patients contemplating surgery, but generally stuck to the interests of the group. The audience overwhelmingly thanked him, and several participants made arrangements for consultations. If the surgeon had continued with his agenda as planned, these relationships would not have transpired.

11. Encourage group participation with brainstorming. The rules of brainstorming include any and all ideas, without judgments. Most certainly a few ideas will attract a few groans and chuckles, but this should be discouraged—every speaker deserves respect and every idea has equal weight.

12. Make eye contact with members of the audience. This creates an atmosphere of conversation and discussion, which is a more favorable listening situation for your audience and a more natural speaking situation for you. Some of the most memorable public speakers I have heard made me feel that they were talking directly to me. One particularly outstanding speaker told me, "I try to make everybody feel like we are all just sittin' around my livin' room havin' pie 'n' coffee while sharin' some new ideas."

13. Highlight the *benefits* versus the features of the product or service you offer. An audience listens more to the *benefits* they stand to gain than the features of the product or service. Use your voice and gestures to underscore these points: how the product or the service can save them money or time (use statistics) and how it is an investment of their resources.

14. Get to the point. Tell people what they need to know. If your audience already knows the problem, you might open with the solution and then expand your comments.

15. **Eliminate distracting speech impediments.** If you have a speech impediment like a lisp, stutter, or strong foreign or regional accent, don't let it get in the way of your ability as a public speaker or group leader. These behaviors may be distracting, but they can usually be treated successfully by a speech-language pathologist.

16. **Summarize the key points at the end of your presentation.** It is your responsibility to be sure your information gets across. Remember in chapter six how your ability to tell back the message is the true test of how well the message was processed? Therefore, periodically—and definitely at the end of a session—ask various students to tell three things they learned. If you let students know that periodic feedback will be a part of the class, they will be more apt to pay attention. This helps students remember the information better and clears up any confusion. This also gives you information about how well you are communicating.

Share Your Movie

1. Take a class in public speaking or join Toastmasters to get practice applying the above suggestions. Seek out a few sessions with a voice coach (contact a university drama school) to help you discover your expressive abilities; be willing to experiment.

2. To determine your average speaking rate, select an article from a newspaper or a magazine. Count out 100 words. Turn on a tape recorder and set a timer for sixty

seconds. Then read your 100 words aloud over and over until the timer goes off. Repeat the exercise two or three times to get a realistic average number of words per minute. Listeners best process information spoken at a rate of 275 to 300 words per minute.

3. Critique your presentation. As painful as it may be, tape a segment of your speech and listen back for utterances like "um," or "uh." Do you repeatedly end sentences with "Okay?", "Right?", or "Everybody with me?" These expressions can seriously detract attention from your message.

Mindful Listening Is Good for Your Health

Listening is an attitude of the heart,
a genuine desire to be with another
which both attracts and heals.

—J. Isham

M indful listening benefits the physical and psychological health of the listener and the speaker. Edward Hallowell, M.D., of Harvard Medical School reported in *Bottom Line* magazine (February 2000) several studies that linked low death rates with feelings of connectedness. According to one study (*Journal of the American Medical Association,* 1997), the most protective factors against violent behavior, severe emotional distress, suicide, and substance abuse among twelve thousand adolescents were feelings of connectedness with family members, schoolmates, and teachers. Several studies in both the United States and abroad involving different age groups support the link between well-being and frequent and positive social encounters. Face-to-face contact with other people has been shown to reduce susceptibility to cold viruses, boost the immune system, and lower pain sensitivity. E-mail and chat lines serve only to increase social isolation.

Dr. James Pennebaker found that when people were given a chance to discuss a stressful event in their lives with willing listeners, their blood pressure decreased. He also reported that having a confidante strengthened the immune system. Being heard lifts self-esteem; we feel important when someone takes the time to hear us out.

Sidney Jourard in his visionary book, *The Transparent Self,* differentiates between inspiriting and dispiriting transactions and their dramatic effects on our health. Because listening is such a powerful connector, it is no surprise that we feel close to our psychiatrists or counselors. *Inspiriting* activities, like being listened to, give us a sense of worth and purpose. Conversely, *dispiriting* transactions, such as failing a test, family arguments, or performing poorly at an interview, make us feel unimportant, worthless, and frustrated. Jourard's hypothesis is that dispiriting events render us vulnerable to illness, while inspiriting ones promote wellness.

Dr. Joyce Brothers (the *Today* show, March 22, 1999) claims that listening to your partner is one of the most important ways to fight fairly when disagreements arise. Unfair fighting (criticizing character versus behavior, cross-complaining, unending accusations, etc.) serves only to depress the immune system.

Dean Ornish, M.D., author of *The Program for Recovering from Heart Disease,* designed a cardiac rehabilitation program with an added feature—group discussions. These groups enable participants from various backgrounds to share their problems with other recovering heart patients. One participant reported his experience:

> It was so interesting to find people from all walks of life with the same basic problems. We all got to know each other as friends with a similar concern—wanting to stay alive. We were above judging each other. Titles, incomes, backgrounds did not matter—we

spoke to each other as human beings with similar problems. I could go to an Ornish group discussion and tell things I would never share even with my spouse. I am convinced this opportunity to be heard and accepted was paramount to my recovery.

Dr. Ornish claims that if we are able to make changes at the psychological and spiritual levels, then the physical heart can begin to improve. On a radio talk show (May 5, 1999, *Fresh Air*, National Public Radio), Ornish suggested that the health benefits attributed to red wine are likely the result of activities associated with drinking wine, namely, lively conversation, the company of other people, and personal disclosure.

Support groups such as AA (Alcoholics Anonymous), or MOMS (Moms Offering Moms Support) are some of the best venues available for mindful listening. Participants share a similar movie, and most of them have experienced many of the same problems. It is the nonjudgmental empathy shared by the group that is often more effective than a session with a counselor who does not share the same experience. A person who is HIV positive is much more likely to be understood by someone else who is HIV positive. Support groups dispel the notion that you are alone, that your anger is shameful, or that you are exaggerating your pain. Participants give each other respect—time to say what's on their minds and hear what works for others.

Those who lead isolated lives experience chronic stress, depression, and decreased immunity. A mindful ear gives a lonely person a chance for self-disclosure and unburdening. This lightening of the load, as crisis counselors will attest, prevents self-inflicting injuries and suicide attempts. Caregivers and patients who participate in support groups have overall better outcomes for survival, are less depressed, and more proactive in directing healthcare decisions.

What makes these groups so health-giving is the sense of

community each member contributes. Most people I spoke to expected to just get information; few expected to experience a connection with the group, and even fewer thought they would want to attend these meetings regularly. The majority agreed that after attending several group meetings, they felt more positive, more eager to contribute to their communities and their friends' lives, and were more patient with strangers.

Dr. Larry Scherwitz found that another risk factor for coronary artery disease is ego indulgence. He noted that when all other factors were controlled, patients who used the pronouns *I, me,* and *my* most often were more likely to develop cardiac problems. Self-focused people, in contrast to other-focused people, are more likely to experience higher levels of dissatisfaction, poorer health, and greater vulnerability to stress.

Perhaps this is what the Zen masters mean by the power of the *sangha,* or group. Zen teaches us that our innate compassionate state would reveal itself more easily if we thought of humanity as one being, one *sangha* with one goal—to help each other get along.

Our dependency on one another may range from obscure to obvious, but in some way, we all depend on each other. For example, the owner of the local hardware store may be the only one for miles who stocks a certain brand of fertilizer that doesn't make you cough or sneeze; your neighbor's dog keeps the rabbits away from your lettuce patch, perhaps the ninety-year-old woman who drives the old blue Nova at twenty miles per hour in a forty-mile-per-hour zone during rush hour is the one who prevents you from spinning out on the oil slick and crashing through the guard rail minutes down the road.

The simple to complex ways that we depend on each other still exist, but gated communities, exclusive clubs, and excessive interaction with computers instead of people physically isolate and dehumanize us. Our great-great-grandparents were master networkers.

Dependency among neighbors and the larger community was the means to sheer survival; each person was a resource. Listening to each other was easy because everyone was in the same boat; barriers and distractions were few and far between. What mattered was the trust established between neighbors, trust built on listening to one another. Nowadays, few of us can name more than three neighbors.

At this point in your listening practice, you may have noticed that you are calmer and less anxious. Not only are you a better listener, but you have also begun to be aware of the thinking and feeling states that influence your ability to process spoken information. Does mindful listening lead to a healthier cardiovascular system?

In *The Language of the Heart,* by James J. Lynch, the author describes a study in which hypertensive patients were hooked up to a computerized blood-pressure monitoring system while they conversed with the experimenter. Blood-pressure readings soared as patients discussed themselves or when their listening became defensive and self-conscious. However, when the experimenter set up a nonthreatening situation by telling the patients a personal experience or reading a passage that helped give a patient another perspective, blood pressure dropped to the lowest levels that patients had enjoyed in years. During these drops in blood pressure, patients momentarily focused on something outside themselves, much like getting into the movie of the speaker. This suggests a connection between our attention mechanisms and the cardiovascular system. Lynch noted the same connection between people and dogs. When you stroke your cat or dog, your blood pressure drops as you temporarily forget yourself and direct your attention to your pet.

Putting aside your agenda and taking the spotlight off yourself is exactly what you need to do when listening under stress. Through regular meditation practice, you can achieve that calm state, set aside your barriers and other defenses, and more directly address the issue. Of course, you may feel strong emotions while listening, but they will not overpower your attempt to understand the speaker and the source of the stress. Instead of wasting time haggling, your meditation practice allows you to clear the mist and get to a solution faster before the stress affects you physically. Epictetus, a first-century Roman philosopher, described the stressful impact of barriers when he said, "Man is disturbed not by things, but by his opinion of things."

Sometimes when I listen in mindfulness to another, it is as if I am in a meditative state. My eyes are open and I am fully aware of my surroundings, but I am totally calm and focused on the speaker. He may make alarming statements, annoy me with his attitude, or be wearing unusual clothes and jewelry that momentarily distract me. Just as in meditation, I note the distraction and gently return my attention to the speaker. When I recognize the mental hijacking in progress, getting back to the breath helps bring my body and mind back to their state of balance.

What exactly happens in our bodies during meditation that allows us to calm down and focus? One theory is that meditation lowers the body's responsiveness to the stress hormone norepinephrine. This theory belongs to Robert Benson, M.D., president of the Mind/ Body Medical Institute at Deaconess Hospital in Boston, Massachusetts, and author of *The Relaxation Response.* In one study, subjects were presented with a stressful situation while heart rate and blood pressure were monitored. Subjects who had meditated twice a day for a month did not experience a rise in heart rate and blood pressure despite a rise in norepinephrine. Subjects who had not meditated experienced the usual increased blood pressure and heart rate. Many programs designed to help people with weight control, coronary heart disease, smoking cessation, and depression now encourage meditation as part of the treatment protocol.

After a day with difficult people, you might think that going home to solitude would be healthy. Think again! In 1998, researchers at Carnegie Mellon University studied the social and psychological effects of Internet use at home. One hundred sixty-nine average Internet users were asked to complete a questionnaire that measured psychological health and featured a self-rating scale that indicated their degree of depression and loneliness. You might assume that Internet users would be happier, since they spend more time interacting on chat lines, bulletin boards, and e-mail. Instead, researchers found a deterioration of social and psychological life. They hypothesize that cyberspace relationships do not provide the kind of psychological support and happiness derived from real-life contact. Professor Robert Kraut claimed, "Our hypothesis is there are more cases where you're building shallow relationships, leading to an overall decline in feeling of connection to other people."

Another concern unique to the computer age is our children. By introducing them to computers at very young ages, are we taking away valuable time needed to develop social skills? Will these computer whizzes grow up to be robotic, communicatively inept beings? According to Jane Healy, author of *Failure to Connect: How Computers Affect Our Children's Minds—for Better and Worse,* "If computer time subtracts from talking, socializing, playing, imagining, or learning to focus the mind internally, the lost ground my be hard or impossible to regain." There is evidence to support a critical period for learning language and social skills, a sensitive sliver of time, generally between the ages of one and seven years. The window of opportunity for mastering computer skills is much greater, as many midlife computer masters can attest. However, during the time between preschool and second grade, children learn to comprehend language, rehearse their sound repertoire, build vocabulary, and acquire the foundation for expressive language ranging from the concrete to the abstract. Coincidentally, this is also the time when children can more easily learn second and third languages. Early conversation practice forms the basis for reasoning, comprehension of complex language, reflection, problem solving, exchange of ideas, empathetic listening, tolerance for different communication styles, and soul building. As parents we must ask ourselves whether computer superiority is worth eroding our children's potential for becoming socially successful human beings.

If you spend a few hours every day communicating with people online, you are getting a taste of the electronic distancing that could become the overwhelming trend in the twenty-first century. It's fast, cheap, and gets a message across. *Which* message is the question. Remember that I mentioned how only 7 percent of thought content is carried by words alone? We derive 93 percent of what a person *means* by gestures, voice tone, and facial expression. Because so much is lost through e-mail or chat-room talk, we are setting ourselves up for a degree of miscommunication and mistrust never before imagined. Might a lack of sufficient face-to-face real-time personal interaction create an emotional fallout that could shorten our life spans? Could we forget how to create meaningful relationships with family members and how to make friends *off* the Internet? Could our people skills become extinct? Might feelings of compassion and caring be only fond childhood memories? Might our children view compassion and caring as an awkward or disturbed behavior? We must ask ourselves, "Is high-tech chat really more convenient and effective?"

Meditation has been shown to quiet the symptoms of anxiety and depression. Unlike medication, however, meditation has no negative side effects, naturally calms the source of the symptoms, and thus eliminates the need for medication. (When meditating, our oxygen consumption is reduced by 20 to 30 percent, which decreases blood lactate levels and results in fewer anxious feelings.)

Physical problems such as pain may inhibit listening. Meditation is reinforced as a way of connecting mind and body for many purposes; listening has been shown to benefit significantly from mind/body synchrony. Studies that show how blood pressure, heart, and breathing rate change as a function of mindful listening. Conversely, the health of speakers is affected positively by mindful listeners. Mindful listening can take place only when the listener's mind and body are balanced. The result is that the listener receives the whole message (words and intent) and processes it to the desired depth of memory. Your daily meditation practice prepares you to experience that mind-body link—your mind is calm, your breathing is slow and steady.

Chapter nine described ways of listening more effectively in stressful circumstances. Mindful listening under stress can eliminate the increased blood pressure and heart rate associated with the fight-or-flight response. Daily breathing practice establishes a higher overall threshold for anxiety, reducing our over-responsiveness to stressful situations. In an emergency, we are more likely to react quickly and intelligently and panic less. Breath control, if practiced regularly, can be elicited at will, which can reduce the activity of the sympathetic nervous system. By purposefully executing breath control, we can make healthful changes in the sympathetic nervous system. With regular practice, the physical and mental changes produced by daily meditation counteract the unhealthy effects of stress.

Most of us value our health more than any car, house, or job. It is essential, then, that both doctor and patient engage in mindful listening. Norman Cousins, a patient who recovered from a near-fatal illness, wrote an article called "The Anatomy of an Illness" (*New England Journal of Medicine,* 1976). His experience emphasized how being listened to played a key role in his recovery. "If I had to guess, I would have to say that the principal contribution made by my doctor to the taming and possible conquest of my illness was that he encouraged me to believe I was a respected partner with him in the total undertaking."

Both parties must take responsibility for the outcome. For you the patient, that means asking straightforward questions, describing symptoms and patterns of symptoms as accurately as possible, providing the most helpful information for the doctor to arrive at the proper diagnosis. You should be aware that most doctor visits may be fifteen minutes or less, so good preparation is appreciated. To make the most of the visit, the doctor should allow at least sixty seconds for the patient to speak without interrupting.

Mindful listening is *empathetic,* not sympathetic. In the doctor's office, as in any consultant-customer situation, empathetic listening means the ability to understand what a person is experiencing. When we give sympathy, we are attentive and reassuring, but removed from the speaker's experience. Mindful listening between doctor and patient creates trust, which has been shown to yield better outcomes from medical treatment. In fact, Dr. Herbert Benson, in *Beyond the Relaxation Response,* claims that trust and a belief in the doctor's advice can "actually alter the patient's physiology—and effect the cure or relief of bodily diseases."

I see this phenomenon often in the clinic. A patient comes to us from an outside medical practice seeking a second opinion. The doctor's advice may be the same as the first opinion, but because the patient felt that he established rapport with the second physician, his symptoms markedly improved even if there was no direct treatment given.

Benson cites a study in which two matched groups of patients were about to undergo similar surgery. One group was visited by the anesthesiologist and given a cursory explanation about the upcoming surgery and a projected recovery time. The second group was visited by the same anesthesiologist, who this time spoke warmly with his patients, listened to their concerns and worries, and answered questions in detail. He also informed them what to expect regarding pain and discomfort during recovery. After surgery, clear differences were noted. The second group recovered sooner and were discharged from the hospital 2.7 days earlier than the first group. That translates into big savings for a hospital. Clearly, our ability to heal can be significantly improved with mindful listening. (It should also be mentioned that mindful listening has, by definition, a positive focus. A patient or customer may not remember everything you told him, but his anxiety and eventual outcome will be significantly affected by dealing with a positive person.)

A doctor's concluding remarks and recommendations should include clarification of medical terms and explanation of side effects of prescribed medications. A responsible patient will repeat back or paraphrase how she understands the recommendations. If time runs out and there are more questions or concerns, some doctors ask the patient to write them down with the assurance that the doctor will call them back at a later time. A visit to your doctor that ignores these crucial points may set off a chain reaction of faulty interpretations, incomplete dissemination of information, misunderstood instructions, noncompliance with treatment suggestions, and—more seriously— a lack of trust.

There is no reason to stay with a physician who is not a good listener. In light of the competitive nature of today's healthcare environment, hospital administrators are becoming more sensitive to the need for patient-friendly physicians. The surge of interest in alternative healthcare such as acupuncture, massage therapy, herbal medicine, and meditation appears to be a direct request from consumers for a more mindful approach to healthcare. Dr. John Abramson, a family practitioner at the Lahey Clinic in Hamilton, Massachusetts, claims that there are two reasons people seek an alternative approach: "People are motivated to use alternative healthcare services for two very different reasons: one is that they are seeking techniques or medications that are not offered in mainstream medicine, but the other is that they desire a different kind of relationship with their caregiver."

The *New England Journal of Medicine* reported that the care and attention delivered in alternative medical practices is causing them to grow by leaps and bounds. Traditional business practices of all kinds would benefit from the implications of this message from patients to traditional medical establishments: people want to be heard, valued, and connected with the decision makers who determine the service or product they are receiving. David Siegel, web guru and author of *Futurize Your Enterprise: Business Strategy in the Age of the E-Customer,* says that customer-driven businesses will be commonplace by 2005. He claims that the way to make the transition from a management-led business to a customer-led business is "First, learn to listen. And listen and listen." Siegel claims, "Markets are really conversations." Can you afford to let distraction get in the way of these conversations?

This book concludes with a story about a king who sought to understand others outside his royal circle. He gave up a life of worldly possessions and false comforts to discover the value of compassion and to share his knowledge with those bound by barriers of prejudice and inhumanity. He listened to and experienced the suffering of others as a way to connect with his fellow human. After several years, he awakened to the reality that we are all dependent on each other to make our lives happy and peaceful, no matter what our status. This man, Siddhartha, came to be known as "the Awakened One" (or Buddha) to his students. He is revered today not as a god, but as a model for patience, sincerity and openness.

Mindful listening in this Age of Distraction is needed as never before for our personal and professional survival. You can choose today to take steps toward understanding your true nature and using your intelligence in a more profound and productive way. The Zen principles discussed in this book—mindfulness, compassion, equanimity, forgetting ourselves long enough to get into movie of another, and meditation—form the basis for truly understanding ourselves and one another. Along the way, like Siddhartha, we can teach others, not by force, but by our example.

Let mindful listening be your guide to continuous self-renewal and compassion toward yourself and others.

Bibliography

Austin, James H. *Zen and the Brain: Toward an Understanding of Meditation and Consciousness.* Cambridge: MIT Press, 1998.

Banville, Thomas C. *How to Listen—How to Be Heard.* Chicago: Nelson-Hall, Inc., 1978.

Benson, Herbert. *The Relaxation Response.* New York: William Morrow & Co., Inc., 1975.

———. *Beyond the Relaxation Response.* New York: Times Books, 1984.

Bolton, Robert. *People Skills.* New York: Simon & Schuster, Inc., 1979.

Burley-Allen, Madelyn. *Listening—the Forgotten Skill.* New York: John Wiley & Sons, 1982.

Buzan, Tony, and Barry Buzan. *The Mind Map Book: How to Use Radiant Thinking to Maximize Your Brain's Untapped Potential.* New York: Plume Books, 1996.

Carew, Jack C. *The Mentor: 15 Keys to Success in Sales, Business and Life.* New York: Penguin Putnam, Inc., 1998.

Covey, Stephen. *The Seven Habits of Highly Effective People.* New York: Simon & Schuster, Inc., 1989.

Crum, Thomas F. *The Magic of Conflict.* New York: Simon & Schuster, Inc., 1987.

Czikszentmihalyi, Mihaly. *Flow: The Psychology of Optimal Experience.* New York: Harper-Collins, 1991.

Dalai Lama and Cutler, Howard C. *The Art of Happiness.* New York: Riverhead Books, 1998.

Easwaran, Eknath. *Meditation.* Tomales, Calif.: Nilgiri Press, 1991.

———. *Words to Live By: Inspiration for Everyday.* Tomales, Calif.: Nilgiri Press, 1996.

Gitomer, Jeffrey. *Customer Satisfaction Is Worthless, Customer Loyalty Is Priceless.* Austin, Tex.: Bard Press, 1998.

Hallowell, Edward M., and John J. Rately. *Driven to Distraction: Recognizing and Coping with Attention Deficit Disorder from Childhood through Adulthood.* New York: Simon & Schuster, Inc., 1994.

Hall, Edward T. and Mildred R. *Understanding Cultural Differences: Keys to Success in West Germany, France and the United States.* Maine: Intercultural Press, 1990.

Healy, Jane M. *Failure to Connect: How Computers Affect Our Children's Minds—for Better and Worse.* New York: Simon & Schuster, Inc., 1998.

Herrmann, Douglas J. *Supermemory: A Quick-Action Program for Memory Improvement.* Emmaus, Pa.: Rodale Press, 1991.

Kabat-Zinn, Jon. *Wherever You Go There You Are: Mindfulness Meditation in Everyday Life.* New York: Hyperion, 1994.

Kurtz, Howard. *Hot Air: All Talk, All the Time.* New York: Times Books, 1996.

Langer, Ellen J. *Mindfulness.* Reading, Mass.: Perseus Books, 1990.

———. *The Power of Mindful Learning.* Reading, Mass.: Perseus Books, 1997.

Lown, Bernard. *The Lost Art of Healing.* Boston: Houghton-Mifflin, 1996.

Maas, James B., with Megan L. Wherry, et al. *Power Sleep: The Revolutionary Program That Prepares Your Mind for Peak Performance.* New York: Villard (Random House), 1998.

Maslow, A. H. *Dominance, Self-Esteem, Self-Actualization: Germinal Papers of A. H. Maslow.* Monterey, Calif.: Brooks/Cole Publishing Company, 1973.

Murphy, Kevin R. and Suzanne Levert. *Out of the Fog: Treatment Options and Coping Strategies for Adult Attention Deficit Disorder.* New York: Skylight Press, 1995.

Nhat Hanh, Thich. *The Miracle of Mindfulness.* Boston: Beacon Press, 1987.

Nichols, Michael P. *The Lost Art of Listening.* New York: Guilford Press, 1995.

Revel, Jean-Francis, and Matthieu Ricard. *The Monk and the Philosopher.* New York: Schocken Books, 1998.

Rosenberg, Marshall B. *Nonviolent Communication: A Language of Compassion.* Del Mar, Calif.: PuddleDancer Press, 1999.

Samovar, L. and R. Porter. *Intercultural Communication: A Reader.* 7th ed. Belmont, Calif.: Wadsworth Publishing, 1997.

Schafer, Edith Nalle. *Our Remarkable Memory.* Washington, D.C.: Starrhill Press, 1988.

Shlien, John. "A Criterion of Psychological Health." *Group Psychotherapy.* p. 1–18, 1994.

Spence, Gerry. *How to Argue and Win Every Time.* New York: St. Martin's Press, 1995.

Stahl, Lesley. *Reporting Live.* New York: Simon & Schuster, Inc., 1999.

Stone, Douglas, et al. *Difficult Conversations: How to Discuss What Matters Most.* New York: Viking Penguin, 1999.

Tannen, Deborah. *Talking from 9 to 5.* New York: William Morrow and Company, Inc., 1994.

Watts, Alan W. *The Spirit of Zen.* New York: Grove Press, 1958.

———. *The Way of Zen.* New York: Vintage Books, 1999.

Wolvin, Andrew, and Carolyn Coakley. *Listening.* 5th ed. Dubuque, Iowa: Brown & Benchmark, 1996.

Woodall, Marian K. *How to Talk So Men Will Listen.* Chicago: Contemporary Press, 1993.

Ziglar, Zig. *See You at the Top.* Gretna, La.: Pelican Publishing Company, 1993.

Zimmerman, Don H., and Candace West. *Sex Roles, Interruptions and Silences in Conversation in Language and Sex: Difference and Dominance.* Rowley, Mass.: Newbury House, 1975.

dreams of yearnings and to the wisdom and beauty that are always around us, when we silence the voice in the back of our head and begin to hear. If you haven't yet read this unique and powerful book, buy it today. It is practical as well as profound; it will change your life.

—**Barbara R. Blakeslee,** trainer and consultant;
President of The Blakeslee Group, Inc.

In The Zen of Listening, *Rebecca Shafir explores how traditional mindfulness practices can help us to communicate with more clarity, depth, and meaning. Ultimately, we discover that mindful communication is a doorway to our own selves, and that our communication is enhanced when we become closer to our own basic nature. When we bring our full awareness and an open heart to our lives, we cannot help but communicate more genuinely. If this message were heard and practiced more widely, it would not just change our communication; it would change our culture and our way of life in critically important ways.*

—**Michael J. Baime, M.D.,** Director of the Penn Program
for Stress Management

By listening we drink in our world. To the extent that this innate ability is compromised, however, we become more or less alone, adrift in a sea of distraction and splintered attention, unable to know ourselves or others in our local or cosmic contexts. Rebecca Shafir has written a book about listening that makes clear what is at stake as our world becomes ever more cluttered. And most importantly, she shows us how to open to a quality of listening that enhances our lives and the lives of those we touch with an open and caring presence. It's hard to imagine a greater contribution than that.

—**Steven Keeva,** author of *Transforming Practices:*
Finding Joy and Satisfaction in the Legal Life

Rebecca Z. Shafir, M.A., CCC, is a certified speech/language pathologist, formerly with the Lahey Clinic in Burlington, Massachusetts and now (as of September 2002) with the Hallowell Center for Cognitive and Emotional Health in Sudbury, Massachusetts. She has been a student of transcendental meditation and Zen for twelve years and holds a black belt in martial arts. A popular teacher of communication workshops nationwide, she has also been a private speech and voice consultant for over twenty years and has coached many well-known performers, political candidates, and business leaders.

Her medical advice has appeared in the *Wall Street Journal, Boston Globe*, and *Computer Current*, as well as in local newspapers and Canadian publications. She has written for trade publications and national magazines/newspapers such as *The ASHA Leader, Bank One*, and *Selling Power*. In addition, she has consulted for articles in *O, The Oprah Magazine, Family Life*, and *Parenting Magazine*.

In promotion of the initial release of *The Zen of Listening* (Quest 2000), the author appeared as a guest on over one hundred radio/TV shows throughout the U.S. and Canada. In 2001, *The Zen of Listening* won *ForeWord Magazine*'s Book of the Year of Award in the category of self-help.

She is available to present a variety of programs ranging from keynote addresses to weeklong seminars tailored to meet the individual needs of corporations, health-care institutions, professional associations, universities, and the general public. For more information or to share your experiences with mindful listening, send your letters to:

Rebecca Z. Shafir
P.O. Box 190
Winchester, MA 01890
Website: www.mindfulcommunication.com

The author is donating a portion of her proceeds from this book to the National Education for Assistance Dog Services (NEADS), the oldest continuing program in the country to train dogs to assist people who are deaf or hearing impaired. For more information, write to:

NEADS
P.O. Box 213
West Boylston, MA 01583
Website: www.neads.org

Quest Books
are published by
The Theosophical Society in America
Wheaton, Illinois 60189-0270,
a worldwide not-for-profit, membership organization
that promotes fellowship among all peoples of the world,
encourages the study of religion, philosophy, and science,
and supports spiritual growth and healing.

Today humanity is on the verge of becoming, for the first time in its history, a global community. The only question is what kind of community it will be. Quest Books strives to fulfill the purpose of the Theosophical Society to act as a leavening; to introduce into humanity a large mindedness, a freedom from bias, an understanding of the values of the East and West; and to point the way to human development as a means of service, both for the individual and for the whole of humankind.

For more information about Quest Books, visit www.questbooks.net For more information about the Theosophical Society, visit www.theosophical.org, or contact Olcott@theosmail.net, or (630) 668-1571.

The Theosophical Publishing House is aided by the generous support of the Kern Foundation, a trust dedicated to Theosophical education.